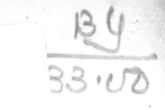

Culture and Management:
A Casebook

Culture and Management: A Casebook

JOSEPH M. PUTTI
Associate Professor of Business Policy
National University of Singapore

AUDREY CHIA-CHAN
Department of Organizational Behavior
National University of Singapore

McGRAW-HILL BOOK CO
Singapore New York St. Louis San Francisco Auckland Bogotá
Caracas Colorado Springs Hamburg Lisbon London Madrid
Mexico Milan Montreal New Delhi Oklahoma City Panama
Paris San Juan São Paulo Sydney Tokyo Toronto

Culture and Management: A Casebook

Copyright © 1990 by McGraw-Hill Book Co - Singapore, 21 Neythal Road, Jurong, Singapore 2262. All rights reserved. No part of this publication may be reproduced, stored in a retrieval system, or transmitted in any form or by any means, electronic, mechanical, photocopying, recording, or otherwise, without the prior written permission of the publisher.

1 2 3 4 5 6 7 8 9 FSP SSG 9 5 4 3 2 1 0

ISBN 0-07-100641-9

This book was set in Century Old Style 10/12 pt
Typeset by Superskill Graphics Pte Ltd
Cover design by Oracle Design

Printed in Singapore

About the Authors

Joseph M Putti

Dr Joseph M Putti is currently Associate Professor in the School of Management at the National University of Singapore. He obtained his Ph.D in Management from Michigan State University in the US and taught and consulted in the US before moving to Singapore.

He has authored several books in Management. Some of them are: Business Strategy and Management, Cases in Human Resource Management, Manager's Primer on Performance Appraisal, Selection: Tips for Managers, Personnel, Understanding Productivity and so on. He has published a number of articles in the field of Management in International Journals.

He is a consultant to a number of organizations in Asia Pacific Region. He has been a guest speaker at many International Conferences and forums.

Audrey Chia-Chan

Audrey Chia is a Senior Tutor in the Department of Organizational Behavior at the Faculty of Business Administration, National University of Singapore. She has an Honors degree in Philosophy. At present she is on study leave at the University of Texas at Austin, pursuing her Ph.D in Management (Organization Science).

Contents

Preface ix
Acknowledgements xi
Introduction xiii
1 The Bonairian "Family" 1
2 Why Marry in September? 6
3 Babalawo and Business Decisions 12
4 The Old-School Expatriate Manager 17
5 The Year of the Tiger 27
6 Mr Suzuki's Dilemma 33
7 Action Aid in Sudan 38
8 Koesmawan's Religious Fervor 44
9 Adelusi is in a Fix 51
10 Good Time and Bad Time at Fina Glassware 59
11 The Progressive Hoe 65
12 Corporate Culture vs National Culture 70
13 Pedro's Cultural Maze 74
14 Goertz's Experience in Thailand 79
15 Mechanization at the Ethiopian Postal Service 83
16 Blood is Thicker than Water 87
17 The Lunar Seventh Month at Allied Service Industries 92
18 Brazil's Too Far Away from Home 96
19 That's Entertainment! 102
20 Intronic's Problem Tree 107
21 Goodshoes (Bangladesh) International 111
22 Hotel le Galant 120
23 "He Will Come Back" 123
24 "After-work Relaxation" Culture in Guyana 128
25 Suryodaya Private Limited 133
26 Lebollo in Lesotho 143
27 The Subordinate Site Engineer 150
28 The Governor Goes Crazy 156

Preface

The twentieth century has been marked by the emergence of multi-national corporations and the globalization of business. It therefore seems quite natural that in recent years, both academics and practitioners have shown increasing interest in management in different cultures. A review of the literature on cross-cultural or comparative management reveals that empirical research studies on various aspects of management are many, but case studies are few.

We believe that one of the best ways to study cross-cultural management is by using case studies. Case studies present first-hand, real-life experiences of managing in different cultures. They can build awareness of cultural influences on management by exposing one to a diversity of experiences which one otherwise might not have. In other words, case studies enable one to practise solving management problems — with all their attendant risks and uncertainties — without actually having to face the consequences of one's decision.

Case studies also provoke one's imagination and encourage one to think not only of theories and formulae, but also of solutions to authentic problems. Another advantage of cross-cultural case studies is that unlike empirical studies, they need not be frequently updated. Cultures evolve slowly and they are relatively stable after they have been formed. Moreover, beliefs, values and other components of culture can be better described and understood qualitatively rather than quantitatively.

Much of the information and inspiration for these case studies is derived from experiences in teaching cross-cultural management and from interaction with executives who work for multinational corporations. From the stories told by these people, their references to specific features of various cultures which they have worked in and from our personal cultural backgrounds, we have developed this collection of case studies.

We have tried to include cases from a variety of cultures, particularly those which may be less familiar because they are seldom mentioned in management texts written by western authors. Some of these countries are Indonesia, Philippines, Thailand, Malaysia, Singapore, Ethiopia, Zambia, Mauritius, Nigeria, Tanzania, India,

Bangladesh, Brazil, Bonaire (a Dutch island off the coast of Venezuela) and Japan.

We hope that this book will be useful for both students and teachers of cross-cultural management, as well as for managers who have to work in a multiplicity of cultures.

Acknowledgements

The authors are indebted to the following experts in the area of Cross-Cultural Management for their encouragement and input in developing this case book:

Professor H C de Bettignies
Stanford University
California, USA

Professor Philippe Lassere
INSEAD
Fontainebleau, France

Professor El-Namaki
International Management Center
Maastricht, Holland

Professor Dexter Dunphy
Australian Graduate School of
    Management
Sydney, Australia

Professor Huang Junyang
Sun Yat Sen University
Kaoshiung, Taiwan

Professor Mitsuyo Hanada
SANNO Institute
Japan

Professor Dong-Sung Cho
Seoul National University
Seoul, Korea

Professor Dharni Sinha
Administrative Staff College
Hyderabad, India

Professor E Soriano
University of Philippines
Manila, Philippines

Professor T Suntivong
Thammasat University
Bangkok, Thailand

Professor James Rosenzweig
University of Washington
Washington, USA

Professor Jack Shapiro
Center for Management, CUNY
New York, USA

Professor Arvind Phatak
Temple University
Pennsylvania, USA

Professor Bob Widyahartono
Universitas Tarumanagara
Jarkarta, Indonesia

Professor Anant Negandhi
University of Illinois
Illinois, USA

Professor Khawaja Amjad Saeed
University of Punjab
Lahore, Pakistan

Acknowledgements

The authors would like to thank the following people for providing material for the cases:

Zewde Abusha
Titilaya Adelusi
Dessie Alemayehu
Jacob Aremu
Arega Beyene
Abustian Elbashir
Cletus Etta
Ir Koesmawan
Khapametsi Maleke
Alexis Matake
Anna Mbede
Charles Mpaulo
Livinus Okpala
Cicely Parris
Zoila Pedro
Orpahaline Saleh
Olajumoke O Taylor
Liping Yang
Tor Tsavar

and other executives and managers who prefer not to be mentioned.

Thanks are also due to Ms Asna binti Abdullah and Ms Latifah binti Wagiman who typed a large part of this manuscript.

Introduction

Cross-cultural management

Comparative management emerged as a distinct field of study in the early 1960s and has since then developed rapidly. At present, one may safely assert that comparative management has gained recognition as a distinct and relevant field of study. This recognition has been given by educators, researchers and managers who have to work amid the globalization of trade.

In education, many schools of business and management — such as the John E. Anderson Graduate School of Management at the University of California, Los Angeles and the Wharton School at the University of Pennsylvania — offer courses in International Management and Comparative Management.

Much of the interest in comparative management has been generated by academics, scholars and researchers who wish to examine management in various cultures. Journals of business and management such as the *Academy of Management Journal* and *Studies in Comparative Management* have generally focused on management practices and problems in different countries or regions. Negandhi (1983) distinguishes among three conceptual and methodical approaches used in studies of comparative management:

The Economic Development orientation which studies the impact of management on achieving economic development;

The Environmental approach which examines the impact of external factors on management practices; and

The Behavioral approach which explains behavioral patterns of individuals and groups in organizations.

The cross-cultural management approach to comparative management is an environmental approach. It explores the effect of culture on the management practices of members of that culture, and inquires into the problems of managers who have to work in cultures which are different from their own.

The growing interest in cross-cultural management has been attributed to Japan's economic success, which prompted researchers to study the effect of Japan's culture on the performance of its companies. De Bettignies (1973) argued that Japanese cultural values such as a deep sense of community, gratitude, willingness to work hard, perseverance and respect for superiors and elders are expressed in the behavior of Japanese at the workplace. Ouchi (1981) contrasted Japanese and American management practices. He characterized Japanese firms as providing lifetime employment, promoting employees more slowly than American firms did, having implicit rather than explicit control mechanisms, using group decision-making (the *ringi* system) rather than consultative or authoritative styles of decision-making and being concerned for every aspect of an employee's welfare. Such practices, Ouchi argued, contributed directly to the success of Japanese companies. Although other researchers (*Child & Tayeb, 1983*) have cautioned against interpreting Japanese management practices only in terms of their culture, they do recognize (*Tayeb, 1988*) that a culture shapes its members' values, attitudes and behavior in the workplace. Tayeb also gives credit to the cultural theory of organizations for acknowledging the fact that cultural attitudes vary in degree across societies and that members of different cultures behave differently because they have different values and attitudes.

Interest in cross-cultural management has also been spurred by the emergence of multinational corporations and the globalization of trade. Managers of multinational corporations need to work in a variety of cultures which are not their own, and with increasing globalization of trade, more and more managers will find themselves having to work in a multiplicity of cultures.

"Culture" defined

The word "culture" has different meanings for different people. In *Images of Organization*, Gareth Morgan describes the way in which the word is usually used:

> When we talk about culture, we are typically referring to the pattern of development reflected in a society's system of knowledge, ideology, values, laws, and day-to-day ritual. The word is frequently used to refer to the degree of refinement evident in such systems of belief and practice . . . Nowadays, however, the concept of culture does not necessarily carry this old evaluative stance. It is used more often to signify that different groups of people have different ways of life.

The idea of culture as a pattern of development is significant. A pattern

Introduction

has regularity of form and consistency, and is often repeated. This means that once one is able to discern the pattern, one will be able to recognize it when one encounters it again. It is also noteworthy that culture is rooted in a society. This society can be a country, tribe, race, religious group, corporation or an organization. Because this is a casebook on cross-cultural management, the culture mentioned in the cases is often of a country, tribe or race. Organizational culture or corporate culture is mentioned in only two cases, *Corporate Culture versus National Culture* and *That's Entertainment!*. In the first case, an organization tries to create a corporate culture with some values which are opposed to the values of the national culture. The second case shows how national values are reflected in the corporate values of Japanese organizations.

Morgan also notes that "culture" is frequently used to denote a system of beliefs and values. "System" implies that the beliefs and values work together as a cohesive whole to produce the practices of that culture. Many of the cases in this book illustrate the impact of a society's beliefs and values on the way its business is conducted, its management practices and behavior of employees. They also show the problems of managers who are alien to the culture or have become alienated from the culture which they once belonged to. These managers do not share the same system of belief, values and assumptions which endow certain objects, actions, times or events with special meanings. For instance, Yahya in *Intronic's Problem Tree* is initially unable to understand the significance of the tree. When he is told of its significance, however, he cannot bring himself to adopt the practice of showing respect to the tree because he rejects the explanation which connects belief with practice. To quote Claude Faucheux (1983),

> A culture is a sharing of common understanding, a common interpretation of the world, a sharing of an accepted view, which makes sense, which gives significance to life, to the whole of human experience as far as memory can go.

Yahya cannot share a common understanding with the other people at Intronic. This understanding is special because it has been passed from one generation to the next, and strengthened by the experiences of each generation.

Because culture is such an enormous and sprawling entity, it

Culture and Management: A Casebook

would be useful to have a framework with which to view it. In his book *Culture and Related Corporate Realities*, Vijay Sathe highlights the fact that cultural anthropologists use the word "culture" to refer to at least two different sets of things. The "adaptationists" define a society's culture as its members' patterns of behavior, speech and use of material objects. To the adaptationists, a society's culture is very much founded on what can be directly observed of its members. The "ideational" school thinks of culture as the ideas, values and beliefs common to the members of a society. Since managers are interested in both behavior and its underlying values, assumptions and beliefs, they could integrate these two definitions, bearing in mind that people could be referring to either types of culture, or both.

However, one cannot really say that one knows a culture if one knows its values, beliefs and assumptions (hereafter referred to as ideas) as well as its practices. One also needs to know how the ideas connect to the practices and how some particular practices manifest some particular ideas. In other words, one needs to know the justification, rationalization or explanation for the practices. This, of course, is based on the ideas of the culture.

The following framework for thinking about culture is adapted from Sathe.

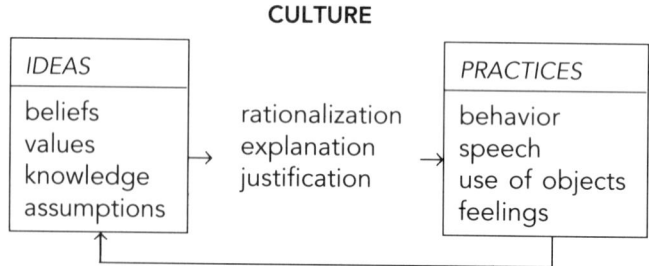

Figure 1. A Framework for Thinking About Culture

We have included the category of feelings under the heading "practices" to indicate that members of a culture may also share feelings because of their common perceptions and ideas.

The culture — ideas and practices — of a society extends to

Introduction

every part of its experience. A society's culture can include ideas and practices about natural phenomena, the world in general, human beings, time, family, gender, objects, animals, dress and appearance, food, language and non-verbal communication.

One interesting feature of culture is that it has the capacity to reinforce itself. The past success of certain practices encourages members of the society to preserve the practices and repeat them. The ideas underlying the practices may also be reinforced. In Figure 1, we have indicated this self-reinforcing capacity of culture by the arrow which leads from practices to ideas.

When one thinks about national or regional culture, one realizes that the factors which affect management practices are not only cultural. Farmer and Richman (1965) have classified these factors as sociological, educational, political and economic. Educational variables, such as the level of literacy and the curricula of schools, influence the quality of the country's workforce. Some political variables are the political stability of the country or region, and the degree of control which the government has over companies. A country's economic health, infrastructure and expectations can also have impact on management practices or create problems for managers.

Thus, while it is wise to consider cultural differences and similarities when thinking about management across cultures, it is equally wise to acknowledge that culture cannot explain all the differences in management practices and the problems faced by managers. Tayeb (1988) has pointed out that some researchers take "culture" to be synonymous with "nation" and suggests:

> Perhaps in future we should be concerned with the cross-national study of management. The change would reflect the view that organizations are influenced by other national institutions besides culture. The term "nation" refers not only to culture but also to other social, economic and political institutions which have a significant bearing on the management styles of organizations located in certain countries.

Objects of Culture

This casebook takes the reader into many cultures. Some of these have similar ideas but different ways of translating them into practice. Depending on whether one takes the ideationist or adaptationist definition of culture, one can say that the two cultures have a similarity or difference.

The cases in this book are drawn from the experiences of managers in a diversity of countries. About half the cases are from experiences in Asian countries — Malaysia, Indonesia, the Philippines, Thailand, Bangladesh, India, Japan and Singapore. Cases from African countries such as Sudan, Tanzania, Zambia and Nigeria have also been included. There are also two cases from Latin-American countries — Brazil and Bonaire.

Reading this collection of cases, one will notice that the objects of culture are many and diverse. They range from intangible constructs such as time to objects like trees and hoes and human beings whether in general or in specific groups such as one's family or tribe. One will also notice that there are some beliefs and values which are held by more than one culture. For instance, both the Chinese and Indian cultures have beliefs about time. The Indian belief that certain times of the day are auspicious or favorable and that other times are unlucky is portrayed in *Good Time and Bad Time at Fina Glassware*. In this case, an employee avoids doing important tasks at "bad times" for fear of adverse consequences, and waits for the "good times" to do the tasks.

The Year of the Tiger is set against the background of the Chinese zodiac. Although the case is based in Singapore, belief in the Chinese zodiac is not limited to some Singaporean Chinese. Belief in the zodiac stems more from racial culture than from national culture. The zodiac assigns an animal to each lunar year, which usually begins in late January or February of the solar calendar. There are twelve animals on the zodiac. Some are believed to bring good luck to the year while others are said to augur ill.

The Chinese belief that certain months are auspicious whilst others are subject to malignant forces is portrayed in *The Lunar Seventh Month at Allied Services Industries* and *Why Marry in September?* The lunar seventh month is, according to old Chinese belief, the time that spirits from the underworld are set free to roam the earth and cause trouble for humans. Some Chinese take this belief so seriously that they forbid their children to go swimming during this month, for fear that they will be drowned by ghosts. The eighth month is considered lucky because the pronunciation of the Chinese character

Introduction

for "eight" (八) puns with the character for "prosperity" (发). Thus, although the Chinese and Indians share a common basic belief that some times are auspicious and others unlucky, they have different specific versions of this belief and different manifestations of it.

The ordinary workday is carved up differently by different cultures; the work week is defined differently too. The mid-afternoon break is part of the Mexican, Spanish and Chinese (mainland) work day. Many foreign organizations and factories in these countries have had to adjust their working hours to accomodate the cultural practice and biorhythms of their local employees.

A cultural value which is prominent in many African countries is respect for one's family and tribe. This value manifests itself in various ways, one of them is preferential treatment of family members and tribesmen, even in the workplace. The rationalization for such behavior is that one should contribute to the well-being of one's family and tribe. The preferential treatment, however, has effects on the recruitment of staff and performance appraisal. This is illustrated in *Blood is Thicker than Water* and *Corporate Culture versus National Culture*. Preferential treatment also affects the quality of service rendered to customers. In *Adelusi is in a Fix*, a manager finds her subordinates giving excellent service to members of their own tribe and neglecting the requests of clients from other tribes.

A number of African and Asian cultures place great value on respect for one's elders. In several African cultures — for instance, Nigerian culture — the elders are given a special greeting. The women kneel (*kumle*) and the men prostrate themselves as signs of reverence to elders. Among the Asian cultures, the Japanese, Chinese, Malays and Indians also emphasize respect for elders. In the Japanese culture, this value extends to the workplace and influences superior-subordinate relations. The value is manifested in the form of respect for one's immediate superior. It is a custom, and one which is accorded much priority, for Japanese employees to visit their immediate superiors on New Year's Day.

Beliefs about gender and gender roles are ingrained in many cultures. The refusal of a Sudanese sheikh to speak to a female representative of a foreign agency in *Action Aid in Sudan* is an expression of how insulted he feels at being made to deal with a woman. The sheikh's culture has taught him that proper women should not work outside the kitchen and home. In *That's Entertainment!* one gets a glimpse of the traditional Japanese idea about women. A Japanese man may marry, but he and his wife may consider it legitimate for him to seek carnal pleasure from other women. Business entertainment, Japanese-style, may not only mean a visit to the bar; it may also include taking one's guest to watch a lewd show.

Different cultures also have different beliefs about human beings. The Bonairians believe that people are generally trustworthy, responsible and honest. Their practices — such as leaving their cars' doors unlocked after parking and not monitoring employees' behavior closely reflect this belief. However, Jason in *The Bonairian Family* interprets such practices as displays of carelessness and gullibility.

The concept of "face" is prominent in several Asian cultures. One's "face" is one's good reputation. The "face" is also the pleasant, decent image which one displays to the world. Maintaining one's "face" or preserving others' "faces", therefore, may necessitate avoiding, suppressing or shielding ugly truths.

The Filipino word for face is *hiya*. People are careful not to "lose face" or to cause others to lose "face". In social interaction, words are carefully chosen and euphemisms used. Diplomacy and tact are used to avoid offending others or embarassing them in public. To publicly draw attention to another's flaws or demand payment for debts would be to cause the other party to lose face. Among the Chinese, too, the "loss" of "face" means personal disgrace in the eyes of the world. To be *mei mien zi*" (没面子) or "faceless" is considered a disaster.

In Asian cultures, people try to "save face" — their own or others' — wherever possible. Face-saving practices may not be compatible with what one has learnt in courses about employee discipline. For instance, a senior manager who is guilty of accepting bribes and who should under the organization's rules of discipline be punished and dismissed might be persuaded to resign "voluntarily" in order to save his "face" as well as the organizations's "face". The case *Pedro's Cultural Maze* illustrates how difficult it is to give negative feedback to employees and enforce discipline in face-conscious cultures.

Culture endows not only people and events with meanings; it does the same for objects. Animistic beliefs, for instance, are part of some cultures. *Intronic's Problem Tree* is about animistic beliefs in Malaysia. In this case, some employees believe that a tree on their company's premises is the dwelling place of a kind and helpful spirit.

Introduction

Hence their treatment of the tree is vastly different from other people's treatment of it.

Animism is sometimes just a segment of a larger body of beliefs in natural and supernatural forces. In Nigeria, the Ibo tribe regards the "Great Mountain" (Ugwu) as a god and worships it accordingly. The mountain is believed to be creator and guardian of the people. The Ibo businessmen and organizations dedicate their work and enterprise to the mountain. Those who fail in their businesses turn to the mountain for recovery and success. The prayer to the Mountain is:

> Great Mountain, we fly to your patronage. Together with our ancestors we acknowledge that you are the Supreme Being, that you are invincible and that you direct us to success in our enterprise. The power of longevity and procreation is yours. We believe that by our respect and constant turning to you in our need, we shall survive the rancour and struggle of this sinful world. We are devoted to respecting your sanctity. We pray for your continued protection and guidance.

Every culture has its epistemic beliefs. Some hold the scientific-rational view of truth. Other cultures, however, believe that science and rationality are not the only ways to discovering truth. Fortune-tellers and prophets have been found in almost every society: the Oracle of Delphi and Nostradumus live on in modern-day horoscope writers, palm-readers, astrologers and dream-interpreters. In some cultures, belief in non-scientific methods of seeking the truth is alive and very much a part of the society. In India and Africa, many people make it a practice to consult fortune-tellers for advice on business or problems at work. The case, *Babalawo and Business Decisions*, illustrates this practice in Nigeria.

Research in Cross-Cultural Management: A quick survey

It has been recognized in other disciplines besides business and management that culture is an important variable. D.F. Lancy (1983) has written on cross-cultural studies in cognition and Mathematics. Sociologists Peter C. Smith and Mehtab S. Karim, have studied urbanization, education and marriage patterns across cultures. The significance of culture is also acknowledged by psychologists; the *Journal of Cross-Cultural Psychology* attests to this.

In the fields of Management and Business, cross-cultural studies are various and numerous. In this section, we quickly survey four cross-cultural studies which have been conducted in the last 20 years or so.

As early as 1966, Haire, et al studied the job satisfaction and fulfilment of motivational needs of 3,600 managers in 14 countries. The needs were classified as security, social, esteem, autonomy and self-actualization. Haire, et al found considerable variations in the reported degree of need satisfaction. These variations could not be explained only by the economic differences among the countries. For instance, the Scandinavian managers reported greater need satisfaction than managers from the United States of America and England although the countries' levels of economic development were similar. Haire, et al also found that managers in the Latin-European countries — Belgium, Italy, Spain and France — gave responses which were similar although their countries were at different levels of economic development. Haire, et al concluded that the pattern of responses suggested that culture did influence the managers' satisfaction.

England (1978) conducted a cross-cultural study of managerial values in the United States of America, Japan, Korea, India and Australia. England found that more Indian managers, as compared to managers from the other countries attached importance to job satisfaction, security power, prestige and individual dignity. Achievement was important to American and Australian managers, and even more important to the Japanese. The Japanese also valued creativity and autonomy. The Koreans attached greater importance to money although they also valued creativity and autonomy.

In a more recent study (1980), Hofstede used four indices to measure cultural differences in work values. The four indices were power distance, uncertainty avoidance, individualism and masculinity. Power distance measures a subordinate's perception of his superior's power over him. Hofstede found that the Power Distance Index (PDI) was highest in the Philippines and Mexico. Singapore had the fifth highest PDI. Taiwan ranked 18th, Great Britain 25th and United States of America 30th. Hofstede's Uncertainty Avoidance Index (UAI) measured the amount of importance which the respondent attached to not breaking rules, his/her intention to stay with the same company and his/her level of job stress. Greece and Portugal had the highest UAI. Taiwan took 19th position, United States of America 31st and Great Britain 34th.

Introduction

Hofstede's individualism measures the relation between an individual and the collectivity in the society of which he/she is a member. According to Hofstede, the degree of individualism varies inversely with the emotional dependence of employees on their organizations. Individualism was found to be highest in United States of America, Great Britain and Australia. It was lower in Hong Kong, Singapore and Taiwan which ranked 31st, 33rd and 35th respectively.

Masculinity (as opposed to Femininity), the way a country copes with its sex roles, is the fourth aspect of national culture which Hofstede examined. On this dimension, Japan and Austria scored highest, Great Britain and United States of America were 8th and 13th respectively, while Singapore and Taiwan took the 24th and 27th places. Hofstede concluded on the basis of the data from earlier studies, as well as data from this study, that in the more masculine countries, the respondent's job is more significant in his/her life than in less masculine countries.

Tayeb (1988) has conducted one of the most recent studies in cross-cultural management. Her comparative study of managers in India and England examines culture, work-related attitudes and organization structure. Some of her findings showed that relative to English employees, Indian employees had lower perception of power, higher uncertainty avoidance (lower tolerance for ambiguity), higher satisfaction with their organizations and more directive attitudes to management practices. Tayeb asserted that these findings reflect the fact that Indians, relative to the English, are more obedient to authority and seniors, less able to cope with change and uncertainty, more fatalistic and more directive than participative in their management styles. However, Tayeb also found that the level of commitment, individualism and interpersonal trust among the Indians and English was similar. The English had higher scores on individualism while the Indians were more collectivistic.

With regard to structure, the survey results showed that English managers delegated their decision-making powers to lower levels of the hierarchy than did the Indian managers. The patterns of communication in English and Indian organizations were consistent with their respective differences in attitudes to management practices.

Cases

More than just recognizing cultural differences, managers have to learn to cope with managing in a diversity of cultures. The skill of managing in different cultures comes largely from exposure to cultures. Management educators, however, can help managers by exposing them to a variety of cultures in the classroom. This can be done by role-plays, discussions with people who belong to various cultures, and case studies. This book is dedicated to the last method of instruction. Some of the cases can even be role-played in class. The chief advantage of cases is that they enable one to immerse oneself in a problem in cross-cultural management and solve the problem as if one were really experiencing it, without having to literally face the consequences of one's chosen solution. The resulting class discussion also helps develop awareness of different perspectives which may be taken. This book is dedicated to all who have to manage cross-culturally, and to all students and educators of cross-cultural management.

1

The Bonairian "Family"

Jason ("Jay") and Wheels

After graduating from an MBA course in the University of California, Jason Sharp joined Wheels, a vehicle rental agency, as a senior executive. Jason (Jay) was pleased to get this job as Wheels was the largest vehicle rental agency in the world. It has more than a thousand agency offices in almost every part of the world, with divisions in North and South America, Europe, East Asia, South-East Asia, Africa, India, Australia, New Zealand and the Middle-East.

Jay's office was in the San Francisco agency. Within three years of appointment, Jay was promoted to assistant agency manager and then to agency manager two years later. Jay's boss, Tony Farmer, the Californian regional manager, often praised Jay for his initiative and commitment to his work. "He's a no-nonsense guy. Some might find him aloof but he keeps the agency in order. Productivity is high and the employees are all disciplined and hardworking," was Tony's favorite description of Jay.

The Invitation

In his third year as agency manager, Jay was invited to Tony's office in Los Angeles for "an important meeting in two days time". Slightly puzzled, Jay wondered why Tony had not given him any information about the matters to be discussed and why the meeting had been called at such short notice.

When he arrived at Tony's office, Jay was surprised to find that the meeting was between Tony and him only. Tony welcomed Jay warmly, and Jay soon learnt the purpose of the meeting.

"As you know, Jay, Wheels opened its first agency in Bonaire six months ago. The agency is barely surviving. Well, we didn't expect the Bonairian agency to do very well. After all, Bonaire is a small place," explained Tony. "And it was in line with the Wheels philosophy that *wheels is where you are* that the agency was set up" added Jay. "Correct," Tony nodded. "But now that the agency's having problems, we need someone to help. How about spending half a year in Bonaire, Jay, to put things right?"

During the rest of the meeting, Tony shared his perception of the problem with Jay. The problem was not competition or poor demand for vehicle rental services. There was no other vehicle rental agency in Bonaire besides Wheels and Bonaire had numerous tourists who created a big demand for rental cars. Yet, the agency was not making money.

Tony then stated that if Jay did decide to accept the appointment in Bonaire, he would be given the title 'Regional Consultant' and represent the regional managers of California and Venezuela. His job was to identify the problems and solve them together with the manager of the Bonairian agency. During the six months, he would draw a monthly salary which was US $500 more than his present salary. On completion of his assignment, Jay could choose either to return to the San Francisco agency or join the regional office as assistant regional manager.

Jay was flattered. From the time he was four, he had dreamt of being a hero. Now, thirty-one years later, he had his chance. Besides, here was a good way to get promoted.

Back in the San Francisco agency, Jay asked his secretary to give him information about Bonaire. Here is a summary of the secretary's report:

> Bonaire is a Carribean island off the coast of Venezuela. The island has an area of 288 km and a population of around 10,000 people. The capital of Bonaire is Kralendijk. Most of Bonaire's population live in Kralendijk or Rincon, a Southern town. Almost

The Bonairian Family

all Bonairians are literate. The four main languages used in Bonaire are Dutch, English, Spanish and Papiamento, the local language.

Catholicism is a major religion in Bonaire. Therefore, superstition hardly plays a role in the lives of Bonairians. The Bonairian economy is largely based on tourism and solar salt production. The standard of living in Bonaire is relatively higher than that of many South American countries.

Two weeks later, on 23 May 1988, Jay left California for Bonaire.

In Bonaire

Jay found the Bonairians incredibly friendly. John, the manager of the Bonairian agency, addressed him as "Jay, my *compader* (friend)". The executives of the agency were so hospitable that they took turns to invite him home for dinner. Jay enjoyed all the attention he received. He got to know the executives' friends and relatives, and even friends of their friends.

After a week of "orientation", Jay stepped into the Wheels agency office for his first day as regional advisor. He noticed that the same friendliness which had characterized those social gatherings was also present in the agency. All employees — whether executives, secretaries, drivers or technicians — were helpful, courteous and accommodating.

During his walk around the agency premises, Jay's hawk-eyed observation told him the following:

* The rental vehicles were left unlocked and the gate to the carpark was also left open.
* The front-office clerks — who were in charge of welcoming customers and taking their orders both personally and on the telephone — tended to talk a lot among themselves and cluster together.
* One or two employees came to work late, but no one seemed to mind, not even their superiors.

Taking stock of his first few days as advisor, Jay felt rather uncomfortable. The friendliness in the work atmosphere bothered him. It was excessive and made the agency look unprofessional. And why were the drivers so careless as to leave the vehicles unlocked? Why, for that matter, was the gate left wide open? Discipline seemed too lax for his liking. Medical leave was approved even when unsupported by a doctor's letter. And why were the latecomers not warned?

Jay decided to speak to John about his observations. When John heard what Jay had to say, he looked surprised and replied, "Oh my *compader*, that is the way things are done around here. None of the vehicles has been stolen so far. We don't lock our own cars either. We have to trust other people. They are all part of the Bonairian family. If the workers come in late, they must have a good reason."

Another aspect of the agency's operations which Jay found disturbing was the drivers' job. The drivers were employed not only to chauffeur clients but also to deliver the vehicles to clients at times and places specified by the clients. In the vehicle rental agreement it was stated that the client would be provided with half a tank of petrol. It was the driver's job to ensure this. Jay realized that the drivers had control of the amount of petrol which could be pumped into each vehicle. The petrol stations simply kept a record of the amount pumped by the drivers and sent a consolidated petrol bill to the agency at the end of each month. "Isn't there a way to check our expenditure on gas?" Jay asked John. "But we can't do that," John almost apologetically said, "The drivers will be offended. We have to trust them. Bonaire is such a small place; I've known some of the drivers since I was a teenager. One or two are my distant relatives. It would be difficult for me to check on them. Let's trust them. I know they are trustworthy."

The Incident

Jay agonized over the problems he had discovered. The next day he awoke with a blocked nose, sore throat and fever. He called the agency to inform John, and went to see a doctor in town.

As Jay drove to the clinic, he noticed that the car in front of his was one of Wheels's cars. The driver had a few local passengers in the car — a woman and two children. The children got off the car when it reached a school. Jay felt suspicious. He believed that the driver was making use of the agency's car and petrol for his personal use. He overtook the car and took a good look at the driver. The latter did not notice Jay at all, and continued talking animatedly to the woman.

Jay felt the impulse to drive straight to the agency and confront the driver when he came to work. But he restrained his anger and decided that it would be better to see the doctor first. Many thoughts

The Bonairian Family

competed for attention in his fevered mind. No wonder the agency was not making money! There were no proper records and control. The people seemed so unprofessional and importing personal relations to the workplace. Jay was not sure what he should do to eradicate all these problems.

As he stepped out of the clinic, Jay decided that he must take immediate action. Despite his illness, he drove quickly to the office. John was summoned to his room.

"Do you know what I saw today?" Jay asked, his voice rising with irritation, "Those drivers — you said we could trust them. Well, we can't. I saw one of them using a Wheels car as if it were his own — driving kids to school, driving his wife to the market. Yes, I've got the car number and I know who the driver is. What we need here is control — we need to tighten up!"

Despite protests from a bewildered John, Jay sacked the errant driver and issued a circular to all staff, ordering everyone to, amongst other things:

* sign in and out of the office,
* produce a doctor's letter to support medical leave,
* lock vehicles and the carpark gate, and
* maintain "a professional, quiet atmosphere" in the office.

In addition, strict records of petrol purchases were to be kept, and drivers had to clock in and out of the office when they went on their assignments. An executive was charged with the duty of ensuring that the drivers left the agency with only just enough time in advance to get them to their destinations on time. Jay then went home to rest.

When Jay returned to the agency the next day, he was met by a sad-faced John, who tendered his resignation. Then, his secretary told him that all the drivers had walked out of their jobs, and that she was resigning too.

What a mess! As Jay sank into his chair, he wondered what had gone wrong. What would he do now? What was he going to tell Tony?

2

Why Marry In September?

Hull and Wright

In Singapore, there is keen competition among companies which provide consultancy services in accounting, management, information systems and recruitment. Hull and Wright is one such company. Despite the competition, Hull and Wright has acquired an enviable reputation for its information systems consultancy services.

Hull and Wright maintains its competitiveness by employing energetic, well-qualified people as consultants. The Information Systems (IS) consultants are all graduates who were in the top 10% of their class. Their ages range from 22 to 37. About half of them have worked elsewhere before joining Hull and Wright.

The IS consultants work in teams. The Head of the IS Department assigns them to teams as and when the company secures a project. Individual consultants may also be transferred from project to project as and when their services are needed. However, this does not happen often because it can cause friction between project leaders. The IS consultants report directly to the Head of the Department. They also report to their project leader but only for the duration of the project. After each project, the team is dissolved and its members are assigned to different teams for new projects.

The IS consultants work very hard. No work day is shorter than nine hours, and on occasion, they work till two or three in the morning.

Why Marry in September?

They frequently work on Sundays and public holidays. The reason for such long work hours is the keen competition among consultancy companies. Clients usually want a job done in as short a time as possible, thus consultancy companies usually bid for a project using the tightest deadline that they can manage.

Olaf

Olaf Andersen had worked with Hull and Wright (Sweden) for six years when he asked for a transfer to the Singapore office. At 38, he had just divorced his wife and wanted to 'get away' from Sweden for good. Besides, the Singapore office needed more IS consultants, and Olaf was too well-qualified for the Singapore office to refuse. Olaf's Swedish boss was disappointed but he thought it would be better to let Olaf go than have a depressed consultant on his hands.

Olaf enjoyed working in Singapore. He got over his depression very quickly, partly because he was so busy. Olaf was made project leader. He had to work closely with the consultants, many of whom were younger than he.

Olaf noticed that there was a high rate of turnover among the IS consultants. About 25 per cent resigned each year. Some consultants resigned because they were "burned out" and wanted a rest; others left to work in industry. As project leader, Olaf naturally wanted all his team members to work on the project from beginning to end, but sometimes, his team had to bear the heavier workload resulting from a team member's resignation.

The Project

One day, Olaf was summoned to the IS Head's office. The Head of Department was Robert, an American who had been working in Singapore for ten years.

Robert looked very excited when Olaf stepped into his office. "Aah! Olaf! Thanks for coming. Sit down," he said, gesticulating to a chair with a sheaf of papers which he had in his right hand. Olaf became excited too. He knew that Robert seldom got excited about things. "What is it, Rob?" Olaf asked.

This is an excerpt of their conversation:

Robert: A huge statutory board — the Board for Housing — has

	asked us for a quotation for an IS job. Here are the details (waving some colored sheets). Have a look.
Olaf:	(after some time) This looks like a very big job, Rob! They want us to develop an integrated system. Sounds challenging.
Robert:	Want to give them a quotation and presentation about how we'll do the project, Olaf? If we get this one, how our image will improve! These statutory boards don't give jobs to any old company. In fact, it's the first time that they're asking an IS consultant to do work for them!
Olaf:	Yes, we could put a team together and give them a presentation in a week!
Robert:	Really? That's the spirit, Olaf! Tell you what, let's pick the team members together. After a meeting or two, we will be able to decide on alternative approaches to developing the system and we'll probably be able to quote a price too.
Olaf:	Good. Let's start now.

The team which was assembled included some of Hull and Wright's best IS consultants. Some of the team members were:

1. *Gerald,* a 32-year old single who liked to dress in designer clothes and loud ties. Gerald amused Olaf very much by his periodic shifting of his desk and chair for reasons of geomancy. Once, he protested against the repositioning of some large plants because they blocked his view of the sea and, consequently, the flow of luck towards him.

2. *Yee Fan,* who was 29 and unmarried. She complained of being constantly assailed by her parents' questions on why she had no boyfriends, what she intended to do with herself if she became a spinster and so on.

3. *Choon Hong,* an experienced consultant who had a Masters Degree in Computer Science from the California Polytechnic University. Choon Hong was 35, and engaged to be married to Alice, another IS consultant.

4. *Alice,* Choon Hong's fiancee. Alice was 26 and the youngest daughter of her parents. She was

"Mummy's girl". When she first started work with Hull and Wright, her mother could not get used to her daughter's long work hours and missed her very much. Alice and Choon Hong adopted a professional attitude and did not let their relationship affect their work.

Besides the four consultants mentioned above, there were seven others on the team. Olaf, the project leader, brought the total number of team members to 12.

The team members spent four days preparing and rehearsing for the presentation to the Housing Board. They were all highly motivated and excited.

On the day of the presentation, the team went in their smartest clothes to the Executive Board Room of the Housing Board. Their presentation was to be given to the Board's Deputy Chief Executive, the Manager of the Administrative Division and Head of Computer Services. Olaf and his team were warmly welcomed. The presentation lasted forty minutes and the Board officials seemed very pleased with it. They kept nodding and smiling.

After two weeks, Olaf received the good news. Hull and Wright had won the $1.2 million job! Work was to begin in January and to be completed by the end of June. Part of the contract provided for compensation to the Housing Board if the project took more than six months to complete.

A few days later, the Housing Board contacted Hull and Wright with a request as to whether they could start the project two months later, that is, in March instead of January, because there was an urgent manpower reshuffle which the Board had to take care of first. They would still be given six months to complete the project. Hull and Wright agreed.

When the project began in March, Olaf noticed that Gerald, Choon Hong and Alice worked extraordinarily hard. They finished their tasks quickly but worked overtime to complete jobs ahead of schedule. Yee Fan, on the other hand, seemed unwilling to work beyond 8 p.m. Olaf soon discovered the reason. Lately, Yee Fan had a boyfriend who was quite smitten by her. He made amorous telephone calls to Yee Fan's temporary office in the Housing Board. Olaf and the team were tickled by this and good-naturedly helped Yee Fan with her work so that she could meet her beau in the evenings. "We must all help the SDU (Social Development Unit)," the consultants laughed. The Social Development Unit was established by the Government to help single graduates find spouses.

Yee Fan, however, did not want to take advantage of her colleagues' kindness and soon reverted to working till late at night and seeing her boyfriend only on weekends. All the consultants realized that six months was barely enough time to complete the project, so they tried to work at optimum speed.

Towards September

In early August, Alice and Choon Hong asked Olaf for a week's leave in September. "We'll be getting married, Olaf," they explained. "We're really sorry that we have to take leave just when the project's to be finished, but our parents are superstitious and insist that we get married then, on the eighth day of the lunar eighth month".

Alice and Choon Hong explained further that September is the eighth month of the Chinese Lunar Calendar. The eighth month is considered to be an auspicious month for marriage because the Chinese pronounciation of 'eight' or " 八 " makes a pun with " 发 " which means "prosperity". If a couple married in the eighth month, their marriage would be blessed by growth and prosperity. On the other hand, certain months are shunned. The sixth month (July) is deemed unlucky because a marriage in mid-year would last only half a year. The seventh month should be completely avoided because it is the month of the "Hungry Ghosts", the month when restless spirits roam the earth and cause trouble for people. The seventh month is so unlucky that some Chinese forbid any mention of forthcoming marriages or preparation for such marriages during the month. "As you know, Olaf, this is Singapore, not the United States or Sweden. Our parents still have a large say in our lives. Respect for their opinions is a part of filial piety," said Choon Hong. Olaf promised to think about their request and discuss it with Rob. "Maybe we can get one or two other consultants to replace you. Don't worry too much about this. And, congratulations!" Olaf smiled.

Upon reflection, Olaf realized that he was living in a culture vastly different from his own. The next day, Yee Fan came to him with a request to take vacation leave in September. Olaf became worried. "Why, Yee Fan?" Blushing, Yee Fan revealed that she would be getting married to her boyfriend. She then went on to give the same explanation about Chinese superstitions regarding the month of marriage. "I'm not superstitious, Olaf, but his parents are and we'd like to please them." "Do you know that Alice and Choon Hong want to get married in September too? It's going to be a real problem for us," said Olaf. "Oh, I'm so sorry, Olaf," cried Yee Fan, "But I can't help it. And my parents want me to get married as soon as possible. After all, most women of my age are already married." Olaf paused, then replied in a troubled tone, "This is really serious. I'm happy for you, Yee Fan, but I need to tell Rob about this. Let's see how we can help ourselves."

Olaf spoke to Rob on the telephone. Rob was surprised and worried, "We can't let them all go together. Getting three replacements would be difficult. You know, Olaf, these are consultants, not production workers." "On the other hand," replied Olaf, "if we let Alice and Choon Hong take leave, and not Yee Fan, we might be seen as biased. Besides, all three of them of them have given a month's notice, which according to our guidelines, is ample notice."

Just then, Gerald burst into Olaf's office. "Olaf, I need help," he said, looking very upset. Olaf promised to call Rob again, then invited Gerald to sit down. "What's up?" he asked kindly. Gerald excitedly answered, "Thanks, Olaf. Oh, I've just heard that Alice, Choon Hong and Yee Fan want to take leave in September. I need to take leave in September, too." "What?" Olaf asked incredulously. "My brother — my favorite, best, closest brother is getting married. I, as his younger brother, have a duty to help him. I'm also the best man. He's getting married on the eighth day of the eighth month in September. That's why I've been working so hard and rushing my work, Olaf. I really need the leave. I know there's lots of work to be done in September, Olaf. I'm sorry I can't be around. If I'm not given leave, I might even resign. I'm sorry, but I'm desperate."

Olaf felt dazed. Four consultants all wanting to go on leave at the same time? He could almost see Hull and Wright giving a handsome compensation to the Housing Board and being blacklisted by all Civil Service organisations and Statutory Boards. He asked Gerald to leave the room, saying that he would see him later. After Gerald left, Olaf fell back onto his chair, groaning, "Why, why marry in September?"

3

Babalawo And Business Decisions

Nigeria, a prosperous African country, is a federation of 21 states. The country is inhabited by a wide variety of ethnic groups. Each ethnic group has its own cultural beliefs and practices. Some of the common cultural practices include witchcraft, sooth saying and ancestral worship.

Despite the western influence in trade, business, education and religion, Nigeria still maintains its cultural identity. Along with modernity, people still follow their traditional cultural practices. Such practices are even carried to the work place and put into practice in making important decisions or in day-to-day routines. Although one may not find such practices in big business operations, they are a fact of life among individual proprietorships and family businesses. At times, managers would rather go to fortune-tellers for business decisions and advices than engage in complex and laborious strategic planning processes. It is not that they lack knowledge or tools needed for modern management practices but they cannot divorce themselves from the traditional practices. Some may even consider resorting to modern practices and tools as the evil way of doing things.

John Okumabuwa hails from a small village about 100 miles from Lagos, the capital of Nigeria. Due to financial constraints he could not complete his high school education. He worked here and there on some part-time jobs and had meager savings. While he was contemplating on his future moves, he met one of his friends who narrated his good luck gained through the advice of a soothsayer.

In Nigeria, a fortune-teller commonly referred to as *BABALAWO* tells people or organizations about what the future holds in stock for them. In order to predict the future, the Babalawo goes through incantations and rituals.

Managers and administrators in some organizations do not place much emphasis on tools and techniques of management. They would rather go to a Babalawo for some advice on their future course of action on certain projects or business decisions instead of engaging in corporate planning, forecasting and spending hours in discussions. In their view, a Babalawo can predict the future more accurately than these tools and techniques. Thus they have absolute trust and confidence in the Babalawo and implement whatever they are told by the latter. Some managers also consult the Babalawo to help them solve major problems confronting their company.

For instance, an earth-moving equipment distribution company was going through an expansion program due to good monsoons in the region. The company was planning to open up two more offices to improve the effectiveness of their service. They knew that they had to decide quickly before their competitor could acquire the office space and establish contacts with the customers. The management team felt that there was no use engaging in feasibility or cost-effectiveness studies in making this decision. The marketing manager suggested that they should consult the Babalawo to find out how many distribution centers they should open, their size and location. The team decided to seek the help of the Babalawo and invited him to deliver the judgement. The Babalawo pointed out two places on the regional map after going through a ritual and gave some indications on the size of these distribution centers. His decision was accepted and implemented.

These stories and experiences convinced John Okumabuwa to seek the help of the Babalawo in deciding his future. After paying the Babalawo with a portion of his savings, John was able to get his assistance. The Babalawo advised him to go to the capital city, Lagos, where he would one day become a leading businessman, operating a transport company.

At first John could not believe what he heard. But he had trust and confidence in the Babalawo's prediction. In 1974, John Okumabuwa moved from his tiny village to the capital city. With the help of one of his uncles he acquired driving skills and found a job as a taxi driver. While he was on this job, John developed good contacts with businessmen, bankers, wholesalers and retailers with whom he frankly shared his dreams and aspirations while he was driving them from place to place. All of them liked his fine personality and mannerisms and promised to help him in accomplishing his aspirations.

Particularly, Mr Orifi, a self-made entrepreneur, assured John of financial assistance in terms of interest-free loans for a period of three years and guidance in starting and operating a transportation business. John took the offer and bought a truck for hauling goods from the port of Lagos to the hinterland. The business was good and the profits were hefty.

One day, as John was resting in his one-room rented accommodation, he reflected on his session with the Babalawo who predicted that he will be a successful transport company owner one day. John saw the prediction slowly coming through. He never dreamt of going to Lagos, becoming a taxi driver nor buying a truck for hauling goods, yet all these have happened.

Strengthened by his belief in the Babalawo's prediction, John Okumabuwa decided to buy two more trailer trucks, thus expanding his fleet for hauling goods. His faith in the Babalawo paid off. His business picked up and profits increased. Induced by this new inspiration, he bought some more vehicles for carrying passengers across the country. Within a few years from the start of his company, he had built up a vast fleet of buses carrying passengers to all nooks and corners of Nigeria.

Okumbuwa's Transport Company maintained a good safety record and the drivers were very disciplined. Because of these qualities, the passengers always preferred to use the buses operated by his company. John's business became so large that the common man on the street believed that one could not count the number of vehicles owned by his company. Within ten years of start of the business, John owned the majority market share of passenger road transport business. People who had known him from his early days wondered how John could achieve such tremendous business success. They remembered that once, he did not even have money to buy food. Some thought that opportunity combined with his good business sense paid off. His business success became a topic or a case study for discussion in many business schools. John alone knew the real cause of his success.

Babalawo and Business Decisions

In 1988, however, Okumabuwa's Transport Company started to have some problems. Many of the company's vehicles were involved in accidents, some serious ones leading to deaths of several passengers. The number of vehicles that broke down on highways was also increased. All these led to the dwindling profits. The company could no longer get new customers and was fast losing the loyalty of the old customers. John was in great shock. He could not figure out the reason for this sudden chain of events.

A consultant from a local university was asked to identify the cause of this disaster and suggest some solutions to improve the situation. After going through the records of the company and interviewing a number of people in the company, the consultant found that the maintenance of the vehicles was carried out regularly and efficiently. The drivers were also given proper training and were paid much better than any other transport company in the country. He sensed a strong corporate culture built on loyalty and efficiency. The morale among the employees was high. The consultant could not exactly pin-point the cause of this debacle.

John was disappointed and discouraged by the consultants' report. He was not sure what steps he should take to remedy the situation. At this moment, one of his close associates suggested that John should go and consult the Babalawo. In an attempt to reverse this downward trend in the fortunes of his business, the transporter went to consult the Babalawo for advice and guidance.

After incantations and rituals the Babalawo told John that his business was declining because his kinsmen in the village were annoyed with him. They felt that John had forsaken them since he achieved his business success. He failed to identify with them or even visit them. According to the Babalawo, John's business would improve only if he went to make peace with his kinsmen in the village. In the first place, he should have sought the blessings of his ancestors. Since he failed to do this, he lost their protection against bad luck and misfortunes.

Being some years in business John was convinced that his business acumen was the real reason for his success. This acumen combined with his fine personality and opportunity at hand resulted in the growth and development of his business. He knew that he had to work very hard to get the business to its peak and gain the majority of the market share.

John was undecided. He was not sure whether he should follow the Babalawo's advice about improving the company's situation or work out something on his own. On one hand, he did not want to let his ego down by going to the Babalawo and on the other hand, he was fearful that if he does not heed the advice of the Babalawo, his business might collapse.

4

The Old-School Expatriate Manager

Albert Chong arrived in his office on Saturday morning with an empty stomach. He was apprehensive as he stepped into his office after he had heard the news from K C Wong, the Personnel Officer, the night before about the union's decision to take industrial action, including a strike at National Overseas Credit (NOC) Bank. As he settled into his chair, he could not help noticing *The Straits Times*' front page with the heading "BANK STAFF DECIDE TO TAKE INDUSTRIAL ACTION" (see Appendix 1). He could clearly imagine the reaction of his boss when he saw his own name on the front page. He felt that the headline report, despite its brevity, was an accurate reflection of the grouses of the majority of the bank employees.

Albert Chong was the bank's audit manager, and according to his boss, he was the most senior local manager in terms of pay. It was for this very reason that he was pushed into the limelight to try to settle some of the outstanding problems which were then the cause of the industrial action. Being the man in the thick of things, he realized that he had to come forth with some alternative course of actions to diffuse the situation and he could certainly expect his manager, Mr C Stappen, to want him to produce the usual one-page memorandum when he got into his office. He had hardly settled down with his pen in hand when his telephone rang. He instinctively sensed it must be Mr Stappen "Albert, see me in one hour and come up with suggestions on how we shall handle this problem." As Albert replaced the receiver, he had no doubt in his mind what problem Mr Stappen was referring to.

History of the NOC Bank

The NOC Bank is licensed as a foreign bank in Singapore to carry out the full range of banking services (inclusive of taking deposits from the public and disbursement of loans). Thus, it was one of the only 37 full-licenced banks in Singapore. It had a licence to operate as an Asian-Currency Unit in the Asian Dollar market (mainly United States dollars).

The Singapore branch was opened in 1858 and is the oldest existing bank in Singapore. The parent bank was founded in 1824 by the king of a colonial power as a commercial enterprise to service trade in the East. With the development of Singapore as a commercial link between the East and West by the middle of the 19th century, the Singapore branch was opened to handle the import and export trade here. Soon it went into the business of financing trade, which had remained its main business to this day. The group had grown to become an international network, whose size now ranked 25th in the world amongst the banking community in terms of total deposits and assets. The Singapore branch was a significant revenue generator in the Southeast Asian region. The importance of the Singapore branch was a natural choice as the site of the Southeast Asia Regional Office was located in the bank's own building.

The Singapore branch had, through the years, retained a low profile compared to its two other competitors which started out at about the same period as foreign banks. Virtually 60% of its activities were in the financing of import and export trade and 40% of its revenue came from industry and commerce. The branch had always depended on a small number of large institutional clients for its deposits. Up to the end of 1979, it had remained content to let this continue. The bank had hitherto provided financing to clients on the basis of recommendations by comrades who were in contact with the local community (particularly Chinese and Indian). It had tended to avoid property financing although it had its own properties. Its loan syndication activity had been nominal till the end of 1979.

The low profile and lack of an aggressive marketing strategy had its price. As in Appendix 2 (extracts from published accounts) losses

The Old-School Expatriate Manager

were incurred in 1974 and the period 1974 through 1979 had been weak indeed. The consequences of inertia compounded by the oil crisis, especially in 1974 and 1975, were reflected in 1975 and 1977.

In 1979, it lagged behind in market image. While its competitors has gone ahead in founding more sophisticated financial services, it had only just started to computerize but on batch processing rather than on on-line. Its banking hall presented an old-fashioned facade — old typewriters, old desks, and the cashier-in-the-cage system (called the "four-eyes" system) rather than the all purpose counter-teller. Compared to other banks, one employee commented that "it is like working in a museum".

Counter and front-line operations staff

The counter and front-line operations staff were relatively young and consisted of an even number of old and new staff (five years' service being taken as the cut-off point). However, the division of functions and responsibilities was not clear. "Anybody could be called to do anybody's job," said one employee. In the Bills Department, a customer could obtain foreign exchange rate quotations from anyone present, and trade documents (letters of credit and bills financing) could be accepted by any employee. Officers were busy signing documents, and the supervision of subordinates and delegation of their duties to middle-level staff were neither systematic nor clear. It was a case of "do how best you can". As a result, this led to frequent "bottlenecks" and delay in the operational workflow, leading to inefficiency and an almost "permanent" level of overtime. The situation usually became worse with seasonal increase in workload and whenever anyone went on vacation leave. There was no study to alleviate the queuing problem and customers were kept waiting for their cash on pay-day. This was compounded by the four-eyes system — "you pass your withdrawal slip to one counter staff, but receive cash at another place (the cashier)". The result was a great deal of confusion and customers' tempers often ran short on pay-days.

Equipment were old. The Burroughs savings account posting machine (bought in 1968) was virtually an antique and even the checkwriter was often not functioning. Typewriters were the Olivetti Linea 88 manual. The young ladies employed hardly stayed more than a year. "I'm too embarrassed to bring my friends in for a visit," said one disgruntled lady.

The physical environment

The Singapore branch was housed in a post-war building which the bank owned but not all the floors were utilized for offices. The third and first floors were rented out as quarters to foreign nationals or to other commercial offices. The bank's two hundred employees occupied the two floors which held 30 sections big and small. Furniture in the banking hall were more than ten years old and one employee commented that this was bad from the public relations standpoint. The only sign, perhaps, of modernization was the NCR 399 mini-computer which was in fact just an "advanced" accounting machine.

The Asian Currency Unit was started in 1978 and headed by a new trainee officer who had just graduated from the University of Singapore. She was not able to get along with a senior clerk who had aspirations to head the department. There were frequent misunderstandings. The clerk decided to hold a union position and became a full-time salaried Union Secretary at the headquarters of the main union for all Singapore bank employees (bargainable staff).

The personnel function

The personnel function was organized as a section within the Administration Division and staffed by a Personnel Officer K C Wong and a clerk. K C Wong was employed as a clerk and appointed as Personnel Officer in 1977 when his predecessor resigned from the company. He had little or no formal training in personnel and industrial relations. His main function was to prepare the payroll, maintain employee records and sort out applications for employment. He was never involved in employee selection or training.

Recruitment and staff development

The traditional method of recruitment of staff was through recommendation by friends and relatives. As a result, the bank had a number of employees who were related to one another by marriage.

An unhappy officer who was passed over for promotion had complained that promotion to higher positions was not based on experience or skills. A caustic remark was "bright office boys can become clerks". In the bank, those with 25 years of service constituted slightly more than a third of the workforce, and those with five to 25 years of service made up another third.

Job evaluation was non-existent and there were few job

The Old-School Expatriate Manager

descriptions. Performance appraisal carried out on an annual basis was subjective — it was a superior's judgement of subordinates on the basis of certain selected desirable traits like ability to work with superiors, subordinates and colleagues.

Training was mainly "on-the-job" and an officer could not recall the last occasion when an employee was sent for an external course. The more senior staff passed down whatever experience and skills they wished to pass on to the junior staff, and there was no exposure to new or better techniques.

Due to rapid changes in the banking industry and the trend towards computerization and office automation, a policy of direct recruitment of better educated workers was implemented (see Appendix 3 for Employee Turnover). "Pay scales were generally unattractive — at least not enough to attract bright young graduates or the GCE (General Cambridge Examination) 'A' Level holders. There was a tendency for employees to treat the bank as a short-term training ground after which they proceed to greener pastures," commented Albert Chong.

Management and organization

The management style in the bank could be described as conservative — traditional hierarchical structure, bureaucratic, autocratic and tending to stick to status quo, despite the rapid changes being made in the banking system. Although an organizational structure did exist, the actual reporting responsibility did not follow this structure, and as Albert Chong said: "The number one man loves to hear employees' grievances and encourages them to go direct to him, bypassing their superiors."

Communication

For a bank operating on rather strict procedures, Albert Chong felt that there were too many memos used for internal communication. Most officers felt it was necessary to confirm even the most trivial matter in writing. The senior managers were expatriates and as they were employed on a three-year contract, job security was related to the relationship and rapport that were established with these expatriate managers. It was observed that in one or two cases, the job security of a local officer was tied to the tenure of the expatriate's contract. Generally, local officers did not voice comments at the officers' meetings; such meetings were viewed as the process by which instructions were transmitted from above. Face-to-face contact between officers was avoided and inter-departmental communication was through the use of office boys. Confidentiality of documents was also not assured.

A New Chief Executive

In December 1978, a new chief executive, Mr C Stappen, was posted to the NOC Bank, Singapore branch. His working life was spent working with the NOC Bank in pre-independent Indonesia and a post-war posting in Germany. Like most bank officers, Mr Stappen worked his way up through the ranks. His knowledge of the East was limited to his five years spent in Indonesia before 1945.

A few months after he took over the reins of the Singapore office, he decided that the first task was to improve the performance of the bank. As Appendix 4 shows, in September 1979, the cumulative ratio of the total profit before tax to total direct cost of operations (called the exploitation ratio)* had been around 250. In a meeting with the senior officers, he felt that better profit was achievable based on his experience in Germany. He decided on a course of action to improve the system and productivity of the staff. His priority was to proceed with the conversion of NCR 399 to the IBM System 34. For those staff who are used to the manual system, this conversion introduced a threat to job security although a series of on-the-job-training sessions was held to acquaint these staff with the new system.

The high level of errors after the implementation of the new system did not help to boost the confidence of the staff. To optimize the use of the IBM System 34, staggered hours in the Computer Department were introduced. K C Wong was approached by the computer operators to approve a 80-dollar per month shift allowance, but Mr Stappen refused on grounds that the number of hours worked by each employee remained the same. Concluding from his own observations that discipline was slack, Mr Stappen instructed that all staff must sign in when reporting for work. As a result, absenteeism and tardiness were no more common occurrences.

Without consulting his officers, Mr Stappen changed the working hours. Generally, the staff of full-licensed banks finished their working day between 5.00 and 5.30 pm and Saturday was a half working day while some banks worked on alternate Saturdays. For the NOC Bank,

The Old-School Expatriate Manager

the working day finished at 6.00 pm and staff reported to work every Saturday.

As the decision on compassionate leave had not been made, Mr Stappen instructed K C Wong to abolish compassionate leave privileges. Compassionate leave of two days' duration was traditionally given to an employee in the event of death of a close relative. When the union objected to this move, Mr Stappen delegated Albert Chong to settle with the union. In a series of meetings, the union presented a number of other grievances and they were not prepared to compromise on this question of compassionate leave. For example, the Union Secretary claimed that some electrical wirings which were left lying on the floor exposed for several weeks during the renovation of one of the offices posed a safety hazard and he demanded that special conditions for the wirings be installed.

To compound the issue, when a telex operator went on two months' statutorily-granted maternity leave, Mr Stappen instructed that a typist be assigned to do relief telex work in addition to her normal typing pool duties. This typist, who was 45 years old and had no experience in operating the telex machine, lodged a complaint with the union.

Wishing to assert his firm control on the bank, he dismissed two senior officers. One of the officers (who was the husband of the 45-years-old typist) was dismissed when he disagreed with Mr Stappen on the trade financing policy. The other officer, whom his colleagues claimed was a "hot-tempered person", was dismissed when he was not able to complete the computerization effort within the one month set by Mr Stappen.

Albert Chong recalled that in a meeting he had with Mr Stappen, the latter expressed the view that: "Autocratic measures are the only way to shake the bank out of its lethargy. We must recruit better qualified officers as replacements". Mr Stappen felt that what he did was good for the bank and decisiveness was necessary.

The Crisis

Personnel matters were now in two hands — K C Wong's and Albert Chong's. Due to his background, K C Wong was not mentally prepared for this fast changing situation and he confided to a colleague that he was "caught between the devil and the deep blue sea".

As each new action of Mr Stappen resulted in widening the gulf between Mr Stappen himself and the employees, Albert Chong was not able to bridge the gap and the situation was gradually getting out of control. The union which had been relatively docile for years sprang to life. For the last 20 years, the bank and the union had seldom found the need to confront each other.

The Central Committee at the Union Headquarters tried in vain to deal directly with the bank manager whom the union claimed was not familiar with the industrial relations set-up in Singapore. As a result, there was a breakdown of communication and the union claimed that this was caused by the "persistent refusal of the bank manager to meet the Union to resolve outstanding issues".

In mid-August 1979, Albert Chong was given a circular from the Secretary of the Union. The circular asked for the convening of an extraordinary meeting and members were to discuss, amongst other things, a resolution to take industrial action.

Appendix 1

Bank staff decide to take industrial action*

A resolution was passed by 187 members of the NOC Bank, Singapore branch on Friday night to take industrial action, including strike.

This is because talks between the Singapore Bank Employees' Union (SBEU) and the NOC management over outstanding issues related to shift allowance, compassionate leave and relief duties have broken down.

The SBEU spokesman said the bank manager, Mr C Stappen had persistently refused to meet the Union to resolve outstanding issues.

These include a negotiable claim of an $80 shift allowance for employees who have to work staggered hours in the computer department.

The Union is also unhappy over the management's inflexible stand on compassionate leave which is only granted in the event of death of an employee's close relatives and not for other emergencies.

The bank has not cleared wires lying about the premises after renovation, thus posing a danger to employees.

Some employees have been made to do relief duties such as telex work in addition to their normal work.

A SBEU statement said the management and the bank employees have worked closely as a team for the past two decades.

Said the union: The new manager, however, for reasons best known to himself and his superiors, deliberately and methodically set out to destroy such cooperation.

The bank yesterday declined to comment.

*Note on Exploitation Ratio in Appendix 4.

Appendix 2

Extracts of the published accounts of the NOC Bank, Singapore Branch

(S$'000)

For year ending 31st December	1978	1977	1976	1975	1974	1973	1972	1971	1970
Cash & balance with Bankers/Agents	199,258	82,284	94,105	44,220	38,733	33,705	13,811	7,387	2,617
Money at call & short notices*	8,000	1,700	11,010	9,200	6,000	—	—	—	—
Bills receivable less provision	56,559	51,984	50,219	49,031	34,973	39,996	21,011	19,985	18,313
Loans and advances to clients	179,631	142,476	127,225	129,414	109,682	97,661	74,539	65,283	49,754
Current, fixed, savings & other deposits	273,522	186,383	141,156	109,074	70,107	66,422	41,541	55,875	39,692
Deposits and balances of Banks/Agents	176,060	82,264	140,747	130,076	144,193	182,377	41,580	29,319	34,309
Profit and loss (after tax, etc.)	3,932	2,687	2,728	2,697	2,853	2,166	1,243	1,015	762
Head Office fund & reserve	29,731	41,690	21,919	20,772	50,334	54,419	45,471	37,673	1,648

Increase/(decrease) — current year compared to last year

Cash & balances with Bankers/Agents	142.16	(12.56)	112.81	14.17	14.92	144.04	86.96	182.27	
Money at call & short notices	370.59	(84.56)	19.67	53.33	—	—	—	—	
Bills receivable less provision	8.80	3.51	2.42	40.20	(12.56)	90.36	5.13	6.23	
Loans and advances to clients	26.08	11.99	(1.69)	17.99	12.31	31.02	14.18	31.21	
Current, fixed, savings & other deposits	46.75	32.04	29.41	55.58	5.55	59.90	(25.65)	40.77	
Deposits & balance of Banks/Agents	141.02	(41.55)	8.20	(9.79)	(20.94)	338.62	41.82	(14.54)	
Profit and loss (after tax, etc)	46.33	(1.50)	1.15	(5.47)	31.72	74.26	22.46	33.20	
Head office fund & reserve	(28.69)	90.20	5.52	(58.73)	(7.51)	19.68	20.70	2185.98	
Total Assets/Liabilities (incl. Cost.)	776,557	513,327	454,016	470,659	437,503	451,949	169,927	152,877	110,346
%	51.28	13.06	(3.54)	7.58	(3.20)	165.97	11.15	38.54	

* For years 1970-73 included under cash & balance with Bankers/Agents.

Culture and Management: A Casebook

Appendix 3

Employee turnover

As at:	Total Head-count	Resignations Per Quarter			Total	% Turn-over Head-count
		Less than 1 year	1-3 years	More than 3 years		
20 Sept 78	184	—	2	2	4	2.2
31 Dec 78	186	—	3	2	5	2.7
31 Mar 79	190	4	1	2	7	3.7
30 Jun 79	190	5	2	2	9	4.7
30 Sept 79	191	4	4	3	11	5.8

Appendix 4

NOC Bank, Singapore Branch

Exploitation Ratio: $\dfrac{\text{Cumulative Year-to-date Profit}}{\text{Cumulative Year-to-date Total Cost}}$

At end of:	1st Qtr	2nd Qtr	3rd Qtr	4th Qtr
1978	240	230	225	218
1979	303	266	247	243

Note on Exploitation Ratio:
Being in a service industry, 80% of a bank's operational cost is in employee-related expenses. Although these costs are expensed off, the cumulative year-to-date total cost is considered as the bank's investment in assets — human assets. This ratio is similar to the asset turnover ratio used in financial accounting, with the emphasis on profits instead of sales turnover. As this ratio refers to human assets, banks refer to this as the exploitation ratio.

5

The Year Of The Tiger

The Company

Vermeer Electronics is a multinational corporation which is based in the Netherlands. It has operations in Australia, Malaysia, Singapore and Taiwan. Vermeer Electronics produces a wide range of electric and electronic goods, ranging from typewriters to refrigerators, calculators, personal computers and toasters.

In 1972, Vermeer Electronics opened its first plant in Singapore. The plant and Head Office were both in a newly-opened industrial estate called Jurong. At present, Vermeer Electronics has four plants in Singapore and plans to open a fifth one in two years' time.

In Singapore, Vermeer Electronics employs 3,500 people, of which only 32 are Dutch. Among the Dutch employees are the General Manager of Vermeer Electronics (Singapore), the Personnel Manager, the Finance Manager, several engineers, trainers and the five plant managers. The non-Dutch employees are all Singaporean, Malaysian or Permanent Residents of Singapore. Nearly 80% of Vermeer Electronics (Singapore) employees are machine operators.

The machine operators work in teams. They are responsible for assembling product parts and checking the intermediate products for defects at different stages of the assembly. A typical machine operator performs tasks which have one to ten steps, and which are repeated dozens of times in an eight-hour work day.

The operators are represented by a union. The union has cordial relations with the management of Vermeer Electronics, partly because of the Personnel Manager's open, friendly attitude and partly because of the company's relatively generous salaries and incentives. On the average, the operators earn a salary of S$630 a month. In addition, they are paid shift allowances when they work the night shift; and they also enjoy medical benefits, meals at subsidized costs and recreational facilities.

On the whole, the operators are happy working with Vermeer Electronics because they feel that their team leaders and the management really care for them. However, Vermeer Electronics has had its share of problems. This case recalls a series of strange happenings in a particular plant of Vermeer Electronics (Singapore) in 1986.

Seng Meng and his team

Chen Seng Meng was a tall, lanky Chinese man who started work with Vermeer Electronics (Singapore) in 1980. When he was 16, he left school and helped at his father's grocery shop until at 18, he joined the army to serve National Service.

After National Service, Seng Meng decided to work with Vermeer Electronics because he wanted to see the world "outside Dad's business". He joined Vermeer Electronics as a machine operator in its oldest plant in Jurong. This plant specialized in making refrigerators.

Seng Meng was an enthusiastic and untiring worker. He was promoted to team leader in 1983. He had twenty operators, both men and women, in his team. In 1984 and 1985, Seng Meng and his team won the 'Best Team of the Year' award. The award was given to the team with the highest productivity and lowest rate of absenteeism and accidents. Seng Meng and his team had an accident-free record. The team members were all loyal to the company and the team. No one had resigned since they began working with Vermeer Electronics. Work relations were so good that the team members even spent time together on weekends. They would play "mahjong" (an indoor game like chess) and go to the cinema or for picnics together.

On Chinese New Year's day in 1986, Seng Meng and his team members visited one another. Between mouthfuls of candy, biscuits and sweetmeats, the team members talked about the coming year and their hopes for it. Then Linda, one of the older operators, said, "I'm not very hopeful. The Year of the Tiger is not a good year at all." The operators fell silent. There are twelve animals in the Chinese Zodiac and each year is associated with one animal in the zodiac. The twelve animals in order are the rat, the ox, the tiger, the rabbit, the dragon, the snake, the horse, the goat, the monkey, the cockerel, the dog and the pig.

After twelve years, the cycle is repeated. Each animal has its significance. For instance, the Year of the Rabbit is considered auspicious for marriages. Dragon Year babies, especially boys, are highly prized. In Singapore, the birth rate in Dragon Years is higher than in other years. It is an old Chinese belief that the Year of the Tiger is inauspicious. The Tiger is conceived of as destructive, strong and merciless. Some Chinese even avoid having babies in the Year of the Tiger because they fear that their children will have tiger's characteristics. About 50 years ago, this belief was so widespread that some parents either abandoned or gave away their baby girls born in the Year of the Tiger.

Noticing that his team members had become quite uncomfortable, Seng Meng tried to cheer them up by saying, "Oh, but that's only an old superstition. The year will be as good as we want it to be". In his heart, however, Seng Meng could not help but feel troubled. He was a religious man who practised traditional Chinese ancestral worship and believed that one must pray hard to avoid being harmed by evil spirits. In his home, there was a two-metre high, red altar with tablets dedicated to his grandparents and great-grandparents. Offerings to his ancestors — such as food, fruit and flowers were placed on the altar. Sometimes, Seng Meng even burnt "heavenly money" (pieces of coloured paper, printed to look like currency) for his ancestors. Ancestral-worship is an ancient Chinese practice borne of filial piety. It cannot, strictly speaking, be called a religion, but in Singapore, it is somehow blended with Taoist and Buddhist elements. Ancestral-worship is sometimes practised alongside worship of Buddhist deities such as Kuan Ying, the Goddess of Mercy. Seng Meng also believed all that his parents had told him about the Chinese Zodiac, and he even consulted the temple's fortune-teller every year.

Into the Year of the Tiger
After a week of New Year festivities, Seng Meng and his team were back at work at eight punctually. They were all in high spirits and had

quite forgotten about their perturbation at the year of the Tiger. A week later, after their lunch recess, Seng Meng and the other operators heard a loud crash, which was followed by a scream and sounds of splintering glass. Immediately, the emergency bell sounded and all the machines ceased operation.

One of the huge glass panes in the ceiling had fallen. Two operators from another team were badly hurt because they had been working directly under the pane. They were taken to the nearest hospital. Five other workers had minor injuries. Seng Meng and his team were shaken by what had happened. "What a very bad start to the year!" they remarked.

Meanwhile, the Dutch manager of the plant, Clemens Gerardus, ordered an investigation into the glass pane accident. Clemens was worried that the operators might no longer feel safe working in the plant which, after all, was Vermeer Electronics's oldest in Singapore. He could not understand why the accident had occurred. The safety of the plant had always been his top priority, and checks and maintenance had been regularly conducted.

Clemens went to the plant to speak to the operators after the accident. Most of them attributed the accident to 'bad luck'. Clemens did not believe in luck of any kind. He had been an atheist for the past twenty years. His parents had tried to make him embrace Christianity, but without success. Clemens believed in himself, in hard work, in science and his employees. According to him, 'there is a logical, scientific explanation for everything. Sometimes, we're not able to find the explanation, that's all!" That was how Clemens tried to comfort his operators. Of course, he also assured them that the plant would continue to be a safe place of work.

The operators respected and liked Clemens although they did not share his atheistic beliefs. However, they did feel consoled and assured. After all, Clemens had been manager of the plant for the past eight years. Under his management, the Jurong plant had the lowest rate of accidents and absenteeism among all the Vermeer Electronics plants in Singapore.

Tiger's Claws

Three days after the glass pane accident, an operator working on the line next to Seng Meng's had his fingers jammed in a machine. Again, the operators became worried. Accidents seemed to be occurring in rapid succession. Two operators were scalded by steam from a machine. Another operator's foot was fractured after a compressor fell on it. These accidents disrupted work and reduced productivity. Two days later, some operators were struck by a strange illness, characterized by nausea and dizziness. Seng Meng's operators complained that they tripped and fell when moving about, although there were no obstacles in their way. "Someone seemed to be pushing us!" they reported to him. Seng Meng did not believe them and scolded his team members for being clumsy — "Don't keep thinking about bad luck! Don't create a self-fulfilling prophecy!" On reflection, however, he felt uneasy. Maybe something weird was happening.

Then, it was Seng Meng's turn. For no apparent reason, he tripped and fell heavily against a machine. His shirt got caught in the moving parts. Quickly, his operators stopped the machine and Seng Meng was safe.

Seng Meng now believed his operators. As they crowded round him during their lunch break, they explained the accidents in their own way. According to them, there was a *chare* in the plant.

In Chinese, *chare* means a spell of bad luck or presence of evil in a certain place. Traditionally, *chare* is removed by a *lamoloh*. A *lamoloh* is not a monk, priest or temple medium. He is a professional who recites prayers and incantations on occasions such as death or when *chare* needs to be removed. A *lamoloh* is paid hundreds, or sometimes, thousands of dollars for a series of rituals and incantations. Sometimes, a *lamoloh* is accompanied by a band which bangs cymbals and plays drums. The costume of the *lamoloh* is a colored cloak with braiding and wide sleeves which flap about when the *lamoloh* perform dances during the incantations.

Seng Meng was persuaded by his team and other operators to speak to Clemens and request that a *lamoloh* be employed to remove the *chare* from the plant. Seng Meng wrote a short letter of request for a *lamoloh* to which 205 operators appended their signatures. Not all the operators signed the letter because not all of them believed in *chare* and *lamoloh*. Some operators were Muslims, others were Hindus, and Christians or Buddhists.

When he received Seng Meng's letter, Clemens was both amused and amazed. For weeks, he had been anxious about the accidents in the plant. He had tried to dismiss them as freak accidents and coincidences, but had found it increasingly difficult to continue doing so. And now, here was the operators' explanation and solution!

Although Clemens did not believe in *chare*, he felt tempted to try the solution. But who was going to pay for the *lamoloh*? Surely not the company, for how could it justify such expenditure? Besides, the operators who had different beliefs might be offended. Even worse, what if some reporter found out that a *lamoloh* was actually invited to dance in the Jurong plant? The company's image as a modern, innovative organization would suffer. On the other hand, no other solution had been found. Should he discuss the operators' solution with the General Manager and other plant managers? How was he going to discuss it without appearing silly? And suppose the *lamoloh* was actually employed but proved ineffective? What then?

6

Mr Suzuki's Dilemma

Yamato Securities is a leading Japanese securities company, employing about 8,000 people in more than 100 branches both in Japan and abroad.

Yamato's founder based his corporate philosophy on the recruitment and training of high-calibre personnel who are investment experts. He believes that everyone, from the President to the raw recruit, is a sales person.

Annually, 100 to 300 raw graduates from Tokyo and other universities are recruited into Yamato's as trainees. All the new employees are treated as trainees during their first three years with the company. Initially, all of the recruits receive training in the Sales Department and live in dormitories provided by the company.

All the newcomers proceed to the training centre in Tokyo where they are given orientation; but the mainstay of Yamato's training program is on-the-job training (OJT).

OJT is considered vital by the top management as it allows the trainees to develop insight into the needs of their customers, including the nature of their investment portfolios and the risk-taking nature of each individual. Negotiation and sales skills can only be acquired after much exposure through OJT.

Initially, this responsibility was given only to the *kacho* or manager. Most of the *kachos* had at least ten years of seniority and it was discovered that there was a generation gap between the *kacho* and his trainees. The top management concluded that this gap should be narrowed and hence the Instructor System was introduced. Under the new system, employees who have three to five years of experience are selected to guide and personally train recruits, with each instructor being responsible for up to five trainees.

Mr Suzuki is the manager of the Minami branch which is one of Yamato's largest branches located in a new industrial area, 600 kilometres from Tokyo. He has served Yamato for 20 years and now controls more than 100 employees. His reponsibilities include supervision of instructors at his branch.

In April 1981, three fresh graduates, Abe, Ito and Tanaka, were recruited by the Personnel Department in Tokyo and posted to Minami. When they reported for work, Suzuki held a short welcoming ceremony for them and exhorted them to learn fast, saying "From today, you are a member of the Yamato team. I'm very happy to work with young people like yourselves. Please do your best to learn. If you have any problem, please speak to Mr Sato, your instructor, or me."

Mr Sato had been selected as instructor on the recommendation of one of Suzuki's deputies. He had been with the company for four years after graduation and had worked in one of the Tokyo branches for three and half years before his transfer, which was about five months ago, to Minami. The transfer is part of the semi-annual rotation process which gives all employees a wide exposure to Yamato's many activities. He had been staying in the company's dormitories since his arrival to Minami but was planning to move out in two months' time to marry his childhood sweetheart.

Sato was an easy-going person, popular with colleagues but his personnel report mentioned that he was occasionally slipshod in his work. Suzuki was a result-oriented manager, and had found that despite occasional complaints from a few customers on improper documentation and tardy delivery of scrip (shares issued instead of divided), Sato was able to bring in above average sales. Besides, he was the only person who could become an instructor as the others were too senior for this post.

During the next few months, Sato had planned to develop his own business while keeping an eye on his trainees. Within a week of their arrival, Abe suddenly got up and left the dormitory one morning. Both Suzuki and Sato were in the office when the dormitory

Mr Suzuki's Dilemma

superintendent rang Suzuki to report that Abe had packed his bags and left. It seemed that he had called his mother who had picked him up from the dormitory.

Suzuki was disturbed by Abe's sudden departure. From the grapevine, he learnt that Abe came from a wealthy family and was the only son. His father was a personal friend of Yamato's president and had asked the latter to take his son in for training so that he could be toughened and prepared to take over the family business.

Sato was immediately summoned to Suzuki's office. "Did you find anything strange in Abe's attitude?" Suzuki asked. "Well, the trainees have been with us only one week. I can't really point out anything unusual. Besides, the job market is very tight and Abe has probably decided to join the million people or so who leave one good company for another. He'll probably regret it," Sato said calmly.

Suzuki felt that not much could be done except to inform the headquarters of Abe's departure.

The other two trainees, Ito and Tanaka did well. The first lesson in their training program was "how to meet people". Sato gave each a stack of name cards and asked them to call on their prospective customers. They had to meet the president of each company they visited. They were very often unsuccessful, but in the process, learnt a lot about how to behave in front of a prospective customer and the nature of industries located in the Minami territory.

During this period of visiting potential customers, Ito and Tanaka returned to Tokyo occasionally for more lectures and discussions regarding market segmentation, stocks and bonds. Summer was the hot season and most trainees usually slackened in their work; but both Ito and Tanaka were able to bring in new customers. Suzuki kept reminding them that he was a result-oriented manager and was full of praise every time they brought in a new customer.

The heat of summer cooled down with the arrival of autumn. Both trainees continued to perform above expectations. Suzuki was particularly pleased when Ito persuaded the president of Toshikawa, one of the region's largest companies, to open an account in late September. Suzuki had been trying for months to get this account and so far, no one in the branch had succeeded in establishing contacts with Toshikawa. Suzuki attributed Ito's success to Sato's skill as an instructor.

One Saturday morning in November, Ito was absent from the

office. As the office was operating for only half a day, absence was taken lightly by his supervisors who thought he had taken time off from work to attend to personal matters. He was again absent the following Monday.

Sato checked with the dormitory (he had left it since his marriage in June) and discovered that Ito had returned to his home in the suburbs of Tokyo. He alerted Suzuki who immediately asked him to contact Ito. Sato rang Ito and was told by his mother that Ito had severe stomach pains and would have to rest at home.

Suzuki informed the Personnel Department in Tokyo and applied for medical leave on Ito's behalf (this is a common practice in Japan). The Personnel Department sent an assistant manager to Ito's home. He was told that Ito's condition was bad and that he needed at least a few weeks' rest before returning to Minami. This was reported to Suzuki.

Ito was away from work for several weeks and in mid-December, he submitted his resignation to the Personnel Department. Suzuki was both puzzled and embarrassed when informed by the Personnel Department that Ito had resigned.

He called Sato in to discuss the resignation. "I can't understand it. Ito's a good man. He is one of our top trainees. What's he like in the dormitory?" Suzuki asked. "I know you like Ito," said Sato, "but he has always been a loner. He has no close friends, stays in his room at the dormitory most of the time and can't even drink. As you know, we take all our newcomers out to drink after work so that we can get to know each other better; but he doesn't enjoy these treats. After the first few weeks, hardly anyone bothers to invite him out for a drink because he was so quiet and showed so little interest in his colleagues. I think he's a queer fellow although quite good at his work."

Suzuki tried to find out more about Ito but was unsuccessful. He filed a report to the Personnel Department which sent another assistant manager to visit Ito in the hope of getting him to withdraw his letter of resignation.

Ito was at home when the assistant manager called. When told that Suzuki had given an excellent report and wanted him back, he politely declined, saying: "Initially, I had wanted to work in the International Business Division. I decided to join Yamato because its international network is well-known. It also seemed interesting to work in the securities business. At the interview which was held in

Tokyo by the Personnel Department last year, I was told that I had to work in the Sales Division for at least a couple of years before I can be considered for transfer to the International Business Division. I was also told that Yamato's management philosophy stated that sales experience was the basis for all jobs in Yamato and I thought this was a very sound policy.

"The life at Minami surprised me. It was totally different from my expectations, perhaps too different. In the first few months, I tried to persuade myself that this experience was vital for my dreams to come true. In fact, OJT was interesting. I like to meet different people through my job. But I was disappointed with my colleagues at Minami. They were too boring for me. I felt very lonely and gradually started asking myself: "Is this the right job for mè?" Then I decided to come back to think of my future. After much soul-searching, I have decided to resign. Now I have no intention to go back to Yamato. I hope I will be able to find a new job soon as I have just graduated less than a year ago. My resignation from Yamato shouldn't hurt my career."

The assistant manager rang Suzuki to tell him of his visit. Suzuki was puzzled and disturbed by Ito's remarks on the Minami branch. Sitting in his office, he reflected on what he should do next.

Ito's resignation would reflect poorly on the company and Suzuki's reputation as a branch manager. Suzuki felt that Ito's remarks could damage his own career progress as they implied that he did not pay enough attention to the needs of his trainees, an important role expected of every senior manager.

"Shall I go after Ito? Is it better to send Sato or Tanaka to Ito's home to persuade him to change his mind? It might be best for me to go there myself. But I'm afraid that if I go, it will show others that I am weak and I will become a bad influence on other subordinates' attitudes" he thought. The best solution might be to forget about it. But is this the right approach? Ito's case seems quite different from, and more serious than Abe's resignation." Is there something wrong with me? Or the training system? What shall I do?"

7

Action Aid In Sudan

Sudan is a vast country in the north eastern part of Africa. Khartoum is its capital. Like some of its neighbors, Sudan has a number of sub-cultures which provide more specific identification and socialization for their members. These sub-cultures are based on differences in religion (Muslims, Christians and Pagans), geographical area (Western, Southern and Eastern Sudan) and ethnic background. The sub-cultures are further sub-divided according to urban or rural living, income, occupation, education, wealth and other characteristics.

The developmental effort undertaken by Sudan to improve its conditions was not even. Some areas were neglected and did not receive their share of development, especially the remote areas. A British organization called Action Aid came to the rescue of one of these areas in 1985 by raising funds through church activities in Britain. The area chosen for development by this organization was the Nuba Mountain Area.

The Nuba Mountain Area

This area is located in the Western part of Sudan, known as the Kordofan region. The literacy rate in this region is very low. Agriculture is the main source of income. The people in this region are frequently affected by drought. The children are exposed to all kinds of illnesses

Action Aid in Sudan

as a result of malnutrition. The health facilities are inadequate to deal with these problems.

The religious groups in this region consist of Christians, Muslims and Pagans. The people were divided into different clans. Though people belong to different religions, they follow the same norms of a particular clan or ethnic group. They speak different dialects.

The area is divided into the North Nuba Mountain District and South Nuba Mountain District. There was a system in Sudan called the System of Indirect Rule. The hierarchy of the system is shown below.

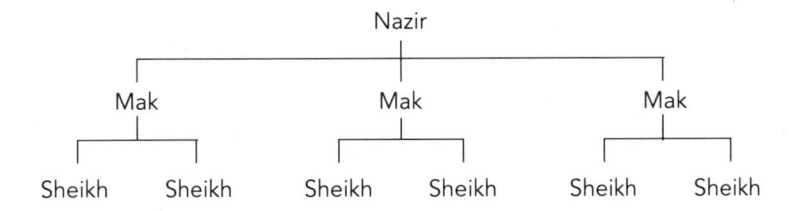

```
                         Nazir
        ┌──────────────────┼──────────────────┐
       Mak                Mak                Mak
     ┌──┴──┐           ┌───┴───┐         ┌────┴────┐
  Sheikh Sheikh     Sheikh  Sheikh    Sheikh    Sheikh
```

A Sheikh is responsible to a Mak or Omda who in turn is responsible to the Nazir. A rural district is placed under the responsibility of a Nazir. A certain number of villages comes under the care of a Mak and each village is further sub-divided into Khahelbaits and placed under the care of a Sheikh. Thus a Nazir delegates authority to a Mak who in turn delegates authority to Sheikh.

Action Aid Program

An aid program known as 'Action Aid' was introduced in 1985 with the help of a British organization to improve the conditions of the people in the rural and remote areas. The churches in Britain contributed to the aid fund and sent volunteers to work in Sudan under this program. The Sudanese government offered its support to this organization in carrying out development activities. It was an integrated development program which focused on the primary needs of people in rural areas, such as starting and maintaining primary schools, health-care centers and dispensaries; providing irrigation facilities and improving agricultural output mainly in the Nuba Mountain area. Besides undertaking project works, loans were granted to farmers who had low income. Prior to this program, these farmers were at the mercy of money-lenders who lent money to the farmers at the beginning of rainy season and collected their repayment in kind at the end of the harvest season. Thus the farmers used to commit a quantity of crops at the time of borrowing. Through the aid program, the government hoped to free the farmers from the clutches of money-lenders.

In order to make the program effective, the organization set up for Action Aid had to rely on formal authority as well as informal authority. The services of the Ministry of Agriculture, Rural District Council and Rural Water Corporation were utilized in exercising formal authority. This was to ensure that there was no bias or corruption in the distribution of loans and provision of services. If this responsibility was totally left to a Sheikh, only a particular clan might benefit and the rich could be made even richer.

The authorities of Action Aid also felt that their work could not be carried out only by the exercise of formal authority. They felt that they needed the help of the Nazirs, Maks and Sheikhs as well. Since the Nazirs, Maks and Sheikhs had direct contact with rural folks, their informal authority and help would be useful when collecting the repayments of loans at frequent intervals. As the Sheikhs were heads of clans, they played a vital role in collecting repayment. To collect repayment of loans, the Nazir passed his authority to the Mak who sent his Sheikhs to collect the repayments.

There was keen competition among the ethnic groups in the various rural areas in the repayment of loans. If a certain ethnic group or clan repaid the entire loan earlier than others, the prestige, status and reputation of that group would be enhanced. Although there was no monetary reward for Nazirs, Maks and Sheikhs, they were considered honest and trusted, and their prestige was enhanced. They received priority in future development projects. The main concern of a Nazir was to ensure that the district under his control was well developed and the people were happy. He made sure that the Sheikhs promptly collected the repayments of loans and there was no misappropriation of money. If the people came to know that their Sheikhs were collecting money for themselves and not accountable to the Nazir, they might refuse to pay back their loans.

The Agricultural Bank of Sudan was instrumental in helping the Action Aid collect the repayment of loans from the farmers. This bank has many branches all over Sudan. The volunteers of the Action Aid agency worked closely with the bank in administering the loans and collecting repayments.

The Joneses

Out of their great zeal for missionary work, Mr and Mrs Earnshaw Jones, both Britons, accepted an assignment in Sudan for the Action Aid program. They had very little knowledge of Sudan but went there with the hope of getting to know the people and their culture in a short period of time. When they arrived in Sudan, they were asked to carry out an assignment in the Nuba Mountain area. It took a week for them to get settled in the new environment and adjust to their new surroundings. Since they had to start their assignment without delay, they did not have much time to learn about the culture of the Sudanese people or the sub-culture in the Nuba Mountain area.

Their assignment required them to visit villages in the Nuba Mountain area, assess the needs of the people, recommend those who were in need for a loan under the Action Aid program and to encourage people to repay their loans so that others could have a chance to get a loan.

Mr and Mrs Jones were given fairly decent accommodation and a jeep to travel in the Nuba Mountain area for their work-related projects. Since they were not familiar with the area, they were given a driver, a local person with a great deal of experience in working with foreigners. The driver knew very little English but enough for daily routine communication.

It was time for harvesting and marketing crops in the Nuba Mountain area. Mrs Jones planned to visit one of the villages so that she could gain first-hand knowledge of the situation and encourage the farmers to pay back their loan instalments. She asked the driver to take her to a village inhabited by a particular group of farmers known as Gashelbait clan.

When she arrived at the village, the driver suggested that she should meet the Sheikh Elbashir first before talking to people in that village. Since the Sheikh was not accustomed to dealing with females in business matters, he asked Mrs Jones to go to his house to talk with his wife and daughters. Mrs Jones was rather puzzled. Out of politeness, she accepted the invitation and went inside the house. She was greeted with smiles, and there was not much verbal communication since neither one understood the language of the other.

Culture and Management: A Casebook

While hospitality was being extended to Mrs Jones inside the house, Sheikh Elbashir was attempting to extract from the driver the purpose of Mrs Jones's visit to the village.

Sheikh: Is Mrs Jones new to Nuba Mountain area?
Driver: Yes, Sir. She arrived only a week ago with her husband.
Sheikh: Does she know much about our area?
Driver: I really doubt it.
Sheikh: What is her job at the bank's branch?
Driver: She is supposed to visit villages, offer assistance, and encourage people to repay their loans.
Sheikh: Is there any specific reason that she has come to our village?
Driver: I thought you knew about it, Sir. She has come to see you regarding loans and loan repayment, I guess.
Sheikh: (On hearing this, the Sheikh became angry and rather nervous). The bank people are insulting me and the people of this village by sending this lady to deal with me on business matters. How can I sit and talk to a *Hurma* (lady)? *Hurma's* place is in *Bait* (house) and not to deal with males on business matters! (Angrily) Tell your bank people not to send anymore of these *Banots* (girls) to us. They will never get repayments. In future we may not take any assistance. Our people may think that this foreign lady is coming here to preach her religion and convert our people.

Mrs Jones did not know what was going on outside and she became restless. She had come to do business and not to drink tea and chat with the Sheikh's family members. She excused herself and went out to meet the Sheikh.

The Sheikh refused to talk to Mrs Jones. He also refused to assist in meeting the village people. Realizing that the Sheikh was offended, the driver rushed Mrs Jones to the jeep and drove off. On the way back, the driver gave her a lesson on local culture and the role of women, especially in the Nuba Mountain area. He told her that the people strongly believed that a woman's place was in the house and she had no right to work outside or impose her views on males. Sheikh Elbashir had been insulted by her visit.

Mrs Jones was in deep shock. Before going to Sudan, she had a good job with a bank in England and enjoyed a comfortable life. She had given up all these and gone to Sudan with the idea of helping the poor. Now she had to face this cultural barrier. She was contemplating whether she should go back to England or attempt to break this cultural barrier. With her limited knowledge of Sudanese culture, she did not know how to overcome this cultural barrier.

The headquarters of Action Aid came to know about the incident. Now they faced multiple problems. They had to find ways of working closely with the Sheikhs so that resistance to the credit program could be minimized. They also had to convince the people and the hierarchy of the informal organization that their motive was not missionary work and conversion. Meanwhile, they decided not to send female volunteers to field work and let them do office work instead.

8

Koesmawan's Religious Fervor

Indonesia, a member of the ASEAN (Association of Southeast Asian Nations) countries, is spread over 13,000 islands and has a population of 170 million. There are more than 200 tribes living on these islands. More than four hundred dialects are spoken although the main language is Bahasa Indonesia.

Despite the diversity of ethnic backgrounds, religious and language barriers, Indonesia enjoys a great deal of unity (*Bhinneka Ika Tunggal*). A commonly used word is "SARA" which is an acronym for Suku(S) meaning tribe; *Agama* (A) religion; *Ras*(R) race and *Antar Golongan* (A) which stands for groups. Put together, SARA means that unity must be maintained at all costs. It is believed that if anything is done to upset "SARA", disaster will follow.

In 1957, there was an incident which disturbed the Indonesians' belief in SARA due to a problem related to *Suku* (tribe). An army leader, Bratamanggala, revolted against the government because people belonging to his tribe (Sundanese) were not given proper representation in civil service jobs while the Javanese tribe was favored. Fortunately, a proper solution was found and the problem was solved before it could erupt into inter-tribal rivalry. The tradition of "SARA" was thus maintained. Similar incidents also occurred due to religious and ethnic differences. For instance, the government had to take timely action and pacify the people when a Muslim leader, Karto Suwiryo, wanted to set up an Islamic state, DI (Darul Islam). The leader created ethnicity-related disturbances between the Chinese and the non-Chinese Indonesians. Despite all these problems, the government could forge a national identity and unity because of its emphasis on "SARA".

The above ideology is supported by the Indonesian philosophy of *Gotong Royong* which means "joint effort". This philosophy is best illustrated by the saying among most of the Indonesians, especially Sundanese and Javanese who constitute about 65% of the population, *Mangan Ora Mangan Kumpul* meaning "whether we have something to eat or not, we join together".

Although the focus is on national unity, some values are of particular importance to certain ethnic or tribal groups. For instance, the value of *Kumaha Engke* of the Sundanese means, "do not think of tomorrow, let us think of today, right now". Thus, they are more present-oriented than forward-looking. The *Alon-Alon Asal Klakon* value of Javanese stresses on completing a job although doing it slowly. The Javenese are not ambitious or concerned about moving fast, but emphasize finishing what they have undertaken. The Padangnese cherish more democratic values. Their principle is *Bulak Aie Dek Pambulah Bulak Kato Dek Mufakat* which simply means "Water flows according to the channel and consensus flows from agreement".

Although 89% of the population is Muslim, Indonesia is not an Islamic State. Islam is not the national religion, unlike in Iran, Pakistan or Saudi Arabia. Indonesia is a secular state but favors all religions. Some of the national holidays include Idul Fitri (Muslims), Hari Natal (Christians), Waisak (Buddhists) and Nyept (Hindus). All religions enjoy rights and privileges.

The country's Charter (Constitution) is based on Five Principles, known as *Pancha Sila* (pronounced as *Panca Sila*). These principles are:

1. Belief in God, the Almighty
2. Humanism
3. Unity
4. Democracy
5. Social Justice

Indonesians take great pride in reading Arnold Toynbee's *East to West — A Journey Round The World* in which Toynbee concludes that Indonesia is the country where five religious groups live in harmony. These religions are Buddhism, Christianity, Islam, Hinduism and Animism.

With such diversity among the Indonesians and the effort of the government to forge unity among them, there are times when certain values of ethnic, tribal and religious groups come into conflict with work in organizations. The case of Mr Koesmawan may be a good illustration.

After graduating from the Industrial Engineering Department of Bandung Institute of Technology, Koesmawan applied for a teaching position at Trisakti University in Jakarta, the capital city of Indonesia. From his childhood, Koesmawan developed an interest in teaching. He was a devout Muslim and felt that a career in teaching would provide him with greater flexibility and not hinder him from practising his religion, especially saying his daily prayers.

As a Muslim, Koesmawan believed in the main principles of Islamic teaching, namely, *AlQuran and AsSunnah*. AlQuran means the Holy Book in which God, Allah, provides directions for leading a good life. AsSunnah relates to the principles laid down by the Prophet Muhamed. One of these principles obliges Muslims to pray at least five times a day. The other principles oblige Muslims to fast during Ramadhan, abstain from eating pork, avoid alcoholic drinks and gambling. Special prayers are offered to Allah on Fridays.

Koesmawan saw teaching as the only occupation that would enable him to practise his religion without any inhibition or hindrance, especially praying five times a day and offering prayers on Fridays in mosques. Although he was a devout Muslim, he did not like to be labeled or identified as a Muslim fundamentalist. From his childhood days, he had friends belonging to different ethnic and religious groups. His friends liked him very much for his soft-spoken manner and the respect he showed for others.

Koesmawan's prayers were answered when he received an appointment letter for a lecturer's position in the Economics Faculty of Trisakti University. His job consisted of teaching Business Mathematics to undergraduate students. He was excited and thanked God for his mercy.

Before accepting the job at Trisakti University and moving to the big city, Jakarta, Koesmawan went to see his father to seek his blessings. His father knew his son's ambition of becoming a teacher but Koesmawan's going to a big city worried him a lot. He was afraid that his son might lose his religious values and forget the training he had received at home when he went to a busy environment like Jakarta's. When he expressed his concern, Koesmawan assured him that he would maintain his strong religious principles and convictions. He told his father that he should not worry about him unnecessarily and that he would keep him informed through weekly or monthly correspondence. His father felt much assured and bade farewell with his blessings.

Upon his arrival in Jakarta, Koesmawan was able to secure some decent accommodation close to a mosque and the university. He was very particular that his apartment should be close to a mosque. The next day he reported to work and was asked to go and see the Dean of the Economics Faculty. Mr Widyartono, the Dean, who was in his 50s, had been with the university for several years. He was a father-figure for his staff. He paid attention to both their academic and personal needs.

Widyartono sensed some special talent in Koesmawan and promised to help him and groom him for greater responsibilities. The Economics Faculty enjoyed a high status and had a good image among the other faculties of the university. This prestige added a special power to Widyartono's position as a Dean. His recommendations to the university were accepted without any questions. In many instances, Widyartono set the trend for the rest of the university to follow.

In his attempts to groom Koesmawan, Widyartono assigned new tasks to him. These assignments included preparing and presenting papers on various projects, attending seminars organized by external bodies and governmental agencies, and representing the Dean in student-related matters. Since he did not have adequate academic training in Business Studies, the Dean obtained sponsorship for Koesmawan to pursue postgraduate studies in Business Administration in another local university. Koesmawan enjoyed his job and benefited very much from the relations he cultivated with the Dean. He earned the trust and confidence of his boss. The close relationship between the Dean and Koesmawan aroused jealousy among members of the Economics Faculty.

Koesmawan took a few days off from his work during the

semester break and went home to visit his father. He narrated his work experiences to him and explained to him how he earned the goodwill of his boss at work. His father was very happy to note that there was no change in his son's religious fervor despite his tremendous success in his work and relations with his boss. After the break, Koesmawan returned to his university.

Upon his return, he found a copy of the circular from the Dean to all the faculty members. The circular read:

> *Effective Friday next week, the Muslim faculty members are requested to pray either in their office rooms or to go to the prayer hall adjacent to the canteen for prayers, instead of going to the mosque outside the university during work hours.*
>
> *The above arrangements would help us to be more effective and efficient at work. We will be available for students to consult us, and the delay in starting afternoon classes would be removed.*
>
> *Any inconvenience caused is regretted. I am sure all of you will cooperate with me in implementing this new procedure.*
>
> *Signed: Widyartono*
> *Dean*

Koesmawan was very upset. His great liking and respect for the Dean turned into anger. People who saw him rush out of his room wondered why he was so upset. His face had turned red, and he was shaking. He murmured to himself, "Why is this old man doing this? All along he was so nice and understanding. What has happened to him? Who helped him to draft this circular?" He barged into the Dean's office and told him that he had decided to resign his job as a result of the circular concerning Friday prayers.

The Dean was rather surprised to see such a behavior in Koesmawan whom he knew all along as an obedient, polite and trustworthy individual. The Dean invited him for a cup of coffee to see whether he could convince him to withdraw his offer of resignation. This is how the conversation went:

Widyartono: What made you upset about my circular when all the others accepted it? I did not expect this type of reaction from you. I thought you would be the last person to object to my circular.

Koesmawan's Religious Fervor

Koesmawan: I respect you very much but I do not have any respect for this circular. I am not sure what or who prompted you to send this circular. You know it is a birthright of every Muslim in this country to offer prayers in mosque on Fridays and you must respect this right. Why did you write this circular?

Widyartono: I am a Muslim too. I understand what you are saying but we have to follow certain rules, regulations and discipline at our workplace. After much thought, I decided to send the circular because things were getting out of hand. Classes were disrupted and students were not given proper attention. Is this principle so important to you?

Koesmawan: Sir, when I took up this job and came to Jakarta, I assured my father that I would keep to my religious principles and that if anything happened to upset them, I would give up my job and return home. The main reason that I accepted a career in teaching is that I thought I would enjoy flexibility. I would be able to perform religious practice without any difficulty. Since this has happened, I do not have any choice but to return home. If my father comes to know of this situation, he will be very unhappy. I do not want to do anything to upset him.

Widyartono: It is my responsibility to maintain discipline and a good environment for students to learn. I do not want to see any disruption in their learning process. This is my responsibility to God. I hope you will reconsider your decision to resign. Come and see me again.

Koesmawan: I understand your position and respect your feelings. I will think it over and see you in a couple of days.

Widyartono: I hope you will have a good news for me then. Maybe we will explore the possibilities of implementing this new procedure in a better way.

Both of them parted on a good note hoping that everything would soon be settled. The Dean was a bit worried that Koesmawan might not show up. Koesmawan's resignation might upset other faculty members. He must be prepared with some alternative strategy within the next few days. For Koesmawan, it was a big decision. On one hand, he did not want to sacrifice his career and felt that he could slowly adjust to the new procedure. On the other hand, the thought of his father and his assurance to him kept bugging him. Neither the Dean nor Koesmawan was sure about who should make the next move. Both were sure, however, that their meeting was going to be sensitive, critical and pivotal.

9

Adelusi Is In A Fix

Nigeria, once an oil-rich country located in the North-Western part of Africa, is somewhat more modernized than many other African countries. Despite its modernization, the tribal structure of the society still seems to be prevalent. There are three major tribal groups in Nigeria. The Ibos originate from the eastern region of the country and are characterized by the values of investing financial resources in male children only, respecting one's own family members, nepotism and expressing themselves through actions rather than words.

The second major tribe, the Havsa, dominated the northern part of the country. The people of this tribe do not show much interest in formal education. The cultural values of this tribe include deep respect for one's wife and show of wealth by the number of children one has. The Yoruba tribe is another major tribe. The values fostered by this tribe include respect for elders, supporting one's parents and the preference for male children.

Though these tribes have certain distinct values, there are some common values that are found in all three tribes and stand out as Nigerian cultural values. These values are loyalty to one's family and identification with one's own village area and inhabitants.

These cultural values strongly influence the day-to-day life of a Nigerian whether he belongs to one tribe or the other. They affect activities and practices in every kind of work organization. While making decisions and carrying out activities in order to implement decisions, these values have to be borne in mind.

The Real-estate Company

Joseph Afalabi returned to Nigeria after getting a Master's degree in Real-Estate in one of the universities in the United States. He explored the possibilities of setting up a business and decided to start a real-estate company. Within a few years of the start of the company, he built up a good pool of clients and a committed workforce. As the business was expanding the number of employees also increased.

In October 1987, Miss Janet Adelusi joined the company as an executive. She had graduated from Ibadan University with a Bachelor's degree in Economics. After interviewing about a dozen candidates, Mr Afalabi selected Janet because she belonged to his own tribe and showed keen interest in the field of real-estate.

Janet was given the title of "Executive — Properties Section" and her responsibilities included keeping record of new properties secured, lettings done by the company, attending to requests of tenants, interviewing potential tenants and property inspections. During the initial period, she was given training by Mr Afalabi himself. She was encouraged to attend short seminars and workshops conducted by the Institutes specializing in real-estate. Given her educational background and enthusiasm for real-estate work, Janet picked up the necessary tools and skills to perform her job effectively. Mr Afalabi was very impressed by the progress she made within a short period of six months and offered her special monetary incentives and perks.

Janet was placed in charge of three scooters and asked to recruit three riders. The main tasks of these riders was to ride around a particular territory or area of the city in which the firm operated, identify new house construction sites and collect information on their completion dates. The riders were also encouraged to approach the landlords to obtain their permission to let their property and provide him with details on service charge and other agreements.

Janet realized that the role of these riders was very important and might determine her own success. She spent considerable time in screening and identifying the potential candidates for the job. She did not want to place an advertisement in the local newspaper because she knew that she would receive hundreds of applications and there would

Adelusi is in a Fix

be tremendous pressure and influence from her own tribal relatives. Through her own contacts with some of her clients and friends, she identified three candidates, namely, Frank from the Ibo tribe, Sola from the Yoruba tribe and Ahmed from the Havsa tribe. All of them had valid licenses and good riding record. They were familiar with the city area.

Janet was convinced that these three candidates would make good riders and went to seek the approval of Mr Afalabi. She summarized the information on her choices and presented to Mr Afalabi in the following manner:

1. *Frank*: Ibo tribe
   Eight years of riding experience
   Single, 28 years old
   High school diploma
   Recommended by a client
2. *Sola*: Yoruba tribe
   Part-time experience since he had to take care of family's hardware store
   Single, 27 years old
   Completed tenth grade education
   Recommended by a friend
3. *Ahmed*: Havsa tribe
   Had been through a series of jobs
   Married, 33 years old
   Studied up to eighth grade
   Recommended by a neighbor

After reading the list, Mr Afalabi asked Janet whether she was convinced that these candidates would do a good job. Janet replied that she was convinced and that she would try them out for three months before confirming them on their jobs. Mr Afalabi approved her choices and left it to her to determine the salaries and incentives.

Janet gave the new recruits a brief orientation and placed them on their jobs. She kept them under personal observation to check their behavior and performance during their stages of adaptation to work environment. Soon she found that Frank (Ibo tribe) was proud and behaved like a boss among the riders because he had longer work experience than the other two. At times, he interfered with the work of the other riders and refused to circulate the current information on properties and other work-related information to the other two. This behavior was annoying to the other riders and created friction once in a while. On the other hand, Frank's work performance was good. Janet waited for an opportunity to deal with this situation.

Sola (Yoruba tribe) spent a considerable amount of time taking care of the hardware store of his family and looking after his aged parents. His attitude and approach to life was unenthusiastic. He was satisfied with average performance in his work and not too concerned about increasing his earnings through incentives. Since he was good-natured and approachable, Janet hoped that she could change his behavior slowly and improve his performance.

Ahmed (Havsa tribe) was the oldest of the three riders and married with three children. In addition, he had to take care of his parents. He had very little education. He moved through a series of jobs trying to find a fit between his interests and education. Janet labeled him as an unstable, crafty and very pretentious person. On one or two occasions, Janet exposed his craftiness and warned him. Although he promised to change his attitude, there was not much improvement except that the frequency of such occurrences were reduced, but not to a significant level.

Each rider had a territory of his own within which he searched for new and available properties. When they secured the properties, they handed them over to Janet on a daily basis. Janet registered the secured properties and sometimes inspected them. Such inspections gave Janet more insights into the property matters, the cultural aspect and the behavior of her subordinates.

The Incident

Frank located a property in his territory but did not follow through when Janet asked him to contact the landlord of the property. Frank claimed that the landlord belonged to the Havsa tribe and he did not want to negotiate the deal with Frank who belonged to the Ibo tribe. He agreed to let the property through Afalabi Real Estate Company on condition that a Havsa tenant was secured. Frank was upset by this incident and decided not to deal with such prejudiced clients in future. Instead of losing the opportunity and to gain some social points, he passed the information to Sola.

Sola was lazy and had difficulty catching up with his own work. He was not enthusiastic about taking up Frank's offer because the property was not in his territory. He felt that Frank was trying to get something out of this deal.

Meanwhile, Ahmed happened to meet the Havsa landlord while he was shopping for a sparepart for his scooter. When the landlord mentioned about the property, Ahmed promised to find Havsa tenants within a week or so. During the conversation, Ahmed came to know that Frank was rather rude to the landlord and passed the information to Sola who never got back to the landlord. Ahmed reported the entire matter to Janet. He twisted the story here and there to Janet in order to create a bad impression of Frank and Sola and gain some favor for himself. He told Janet that Frank felt that he should be the boss of the department since he was much older than Janet. Knowing the craftiness of Ahmed, Janet terminated the conversation by promising him that she would look into the matter. Janet accepted the fact that the landlord was free to dictate who he wanted to have in his property and that the company could not do anything about it.

Janet wanted to contact the Havsa landlord directly and explain the policies and working style of Afalabi Real Estate Company. Since Havsas respect females, Janet thought that she could get the message across to the landlord without any problem. Besides, she had the knack of getting along with all sorts of people because of her ability to empathize. When she indicated her desire to make direct contact with the landlord, Ahmed discouraged her by doing so. He told Janet that in his culture, younger people (Janet was 22 years old) are not given such responsibilities of approaching older people and giving them some important advice.

Janet gave second thought to her intention of approaching the landlord directly and gave the responsibility to Ahmed who was delighted to handle the matter. Ahmed paid a great deal of attention to this particular assignment of finding a Havsa tenant for the landlord and in this process, he neglected other tasks assigned to him. Probably, he was motivated by the expectation of the benefits he would receive from the landlord once he succeeded in letting the property to a Havsa tenant only. He also felt that his status in the organization would also be enhanced because he was able to accomplish something that the other two riders could not.

Driven by his disappointment and anger against the incident

Culture and Management: A Casebook

involving the Havsa landlord, Frank reacted by concentrating on property owners from his own tribe (Ibo), thus ignoring the territorial assignments made by the company. Sola reciprocated in the same way by establishing contacts with Yoruba property owners. These informal arrangements created a great deal of confusion and conflicts even involving other members in the organization. Cultural values of each tribe were reflected in the way the employees carried out their tasks.

Janet came to know that Frank, being an Ibo man, concentrated only on renting properties which he had secured to his close and extended family members and that Sola, being lazy, still found the will to concentrate only on Yoruba tenants and even turned away some potential tenants simply because they were not from his tribe.

As the pressure mounted, Janet felt that it was proper for her to bring this matter to the notice of Mr Afalabi. Janet was worried that her boss might lose his temper and that it would be the end of her career with Afalabi Real Estate Company. But on the contrary, Afalabi was pleased with the informal arrangements being made among the riders because the new arrangement seemed to have a positive impact on profits. Many tenants came to know that Afalabi Real Estate Company served clients from all tribes without any prejudice or bias. Many landowner-tenant related problems were solved because under the new arrangement, proper matchings were done by providing a tenant from the same tribe to the landowner of the same tribe. Time and effort in bringing the tenant and landowner together were also reduced because of the familiarity between them as members of the same tribe.

Gradually, the cultural values of various tribal groups became ingrained and formed a unique corporate culture at Afalabi Real Estate Company.

It was a cultural shock for Janet. The theories and knowledge gained through her academic preparation had to be put aside since cultural forces had taken over the situation. When she accepted the position, she had great ideas of introducing modern management techniques and practices. For instance, she wanted to introduce specific job descriptions for the riders. This would enable them to follow assignments strictly on their territorial allocations. Janet was working on a performance appraisal system for the entire company on the advice of her boss. She was keen on introducing an objective-centered appraisal system and tying an incentive system to it. A training plan for the riders had been worked out to provide them with skills on customer relations and technical knowledge to complete the property deal. She kept her boss informed of all these activities and received full support and encouragement from her boss. Mr Afalabi, himself educated abroad, could see the benefits of modern management practices and techniques. Both had been in agreement that a modern approach must be gradually introduced to the organization.

After having the discussion on the conflicts that were taking place in the department with her boss, Janet returned to her office. She sat there motionless, reflecting on the past encouragement and enthusiasm shown by her boss and the current attitude of letting local cultural practices take over the whole situation and not paying much attention to the introduction of modern management practices and techniques. She contemplated on the future course of action for herself. On the one hand, she did not want to quit the company because she saw a good future there. The present job had been a good learning experience for her. She was also in the midst of developing certain systems and procedures. Janet felt that she could convince her boss sooner or later to introduce her ideas systematically. On the other hand, she was frustrated with the attitude of her boss who did not have the ability to think for the long-term good of the organization and was interested in making quick bucks in the short run.

Janet identified the following options left to her as a result of the chaos at the Afalabi Real Estate Company. She could:

1. Tender her resignation right away, telling her boss that she did not want to sacrifice her professionalism for the sake of respect for local cultural values.
2. Stay with the company and wait for an opportunity to change the situation gradually without upsetting her boss and other employees.
3. Simply go along with whatever was happening currently in the company, accepting the importance of local cultural values and effective forces in the organization. Furthermore, adapting to the forces had yielded good results.
4. Take leave of absence to pursue higher studies in Business Administration. She had been offered a government scholarship to study in the International Management Center in Holland.
5. Modify systems and procedures she was currently working on, taking cultural values into consideration.

Time was running out for Janet if she was going to take up the scholarship or look for a better job elsewhere as the job market was lucrative at that time. Which course of action should Janet pursue, taking the implications of each option into consideration?

10

Good Time And Bad Time At Fina Glassware

Soon after graduating from a Mid-Western university, George Foster joined Fina Glassware — a multinational corporation manufacturing and distributing glassware in about 40 countries around the world. George was from a conservative, Protestant, mid-Western family. He was a devout Baptist.

While he was doing his Master's degree in Business Administration, he produced a project paper titled, "Christian Values in Management". He received "A" grade for his paper. Basically, the paper discussed how the Protestant Ethic of the western nations was implemented and practiced in business organizations. It stressed how an individual should maximize his time at work.

George progressed well in his work, was promoted and assumed higher responsibilities in quick succession. His missionary zeal prompted him to request for an international assignment. The committee set up at the corporate level for screening and recommending candidates for overseas assignment asked George why he had requested for an international assignment, he replied, "I have always had the desire to work in a Third World country so that I can help train people".

George was an efficiency expert. In the past, he designed a series of systems and procedures to improve work efficiency in divisions where he worked. His technical skills and expertise made him ideal for an international assignment. But George's knowledge about cultures, traditions and customs of people in other countries was limited. In the past, he made two or three trips to Mexico for short business meetings each of which lasted for a day or two. After one of his trips to Mexico, a colleague, Bill Watson, asked him how he enjoyed his trip, George replied, "Oh! I love Mexican food. I bought a couple of Mexican souvenirs for a reasonable price". That was the extent to which George was familiar with Mexican culture.

George assured the corporate committee on international assignment that he would acquire published materials on Third World countries and become familiar with their traditions and cultures before taking up an international assignment. When quizzed on the extent of his reading of material pertaining to the Third World countries in the past, George replied "I read a couple of books while I was in my graduate program for a course on International Business. If I can recollect, the titles are: "The Maya Culture" and "Theory Z".

Since not many executives opted for international assignments and George was keen on an international assignment, the committee decided to send George to a Third World country. A choice of four countries was offered to George. The choices and designations were:

Bangkok, Thailand	— Regional Marketing Manager
Lagos, Nigeria	— Plant Manager
Madras, India	— Managing Director of Cookware Division
Lima, Peru	— Head of South American Distribution Center

George was really puzzled by the choice. He told the committee that he would discuss the matter with his wife and convey his choice to the committee within a week. George had a lengthy discussion with his wife, Sheila, who expressed an interest in India. Besides a craving for spicy Indian food, Sheila had a good collection of Indian rugs, jewellery and handicrafts. George was also more inclined towards the Indian choice because of the position of managing director.

All the formalities were completed within a month. George and his family arrived in Madras, facing a new and challenging life ahead for the next three years. It took him nearly four months to get settled in his work and become familiar with the day-to-day operations of the subsidiary.

Good Time and Bad Time at Fina Glassware

The Madras subsidiary of Fina Glassware Corporation employed 1500 people and manufactured cookware-related items. The product line of 20 items ranged from coffee cups to cookware. The manufactured items were sold mostly in India and a small portion was shipped back to the United States. The organization chart of the subsidiary is shown in Figure 1.

George asked Ram Gopal, the marketing manager, to submit a tentative outline for a promotional plan for a new product (a coffee pot) to be released into the market shortly. Ram agreed to see George by 2 pm on the same day with a plan. When Ram returned to his office after his morning meeting with George, he realized that he could not start his work on the promotional plan until 1.30 pm because it was not an "auspicious" time. His Hindu religious calendar, *Panchangam*, showed that it was *Yamagandam* between 10.30 am and 1.30 pm.

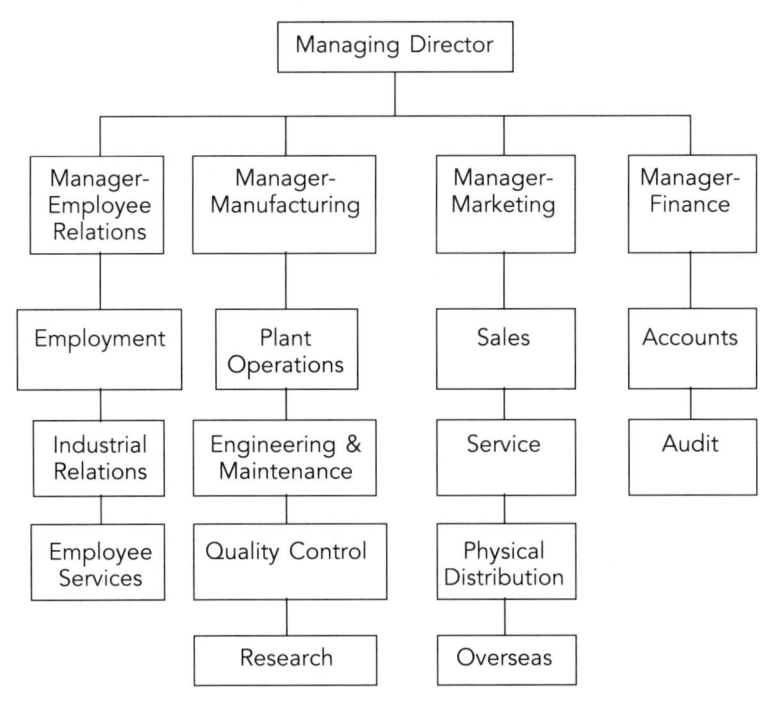

```
                        Managing Director
                               |
   ┌───────────────┬───────────┴───────┬───────────────┐
 Manager-       Manager-            Manager-         Manager-
 Employee       Manufacturing       Marketing        Finance
 Relations
     |               |                   |               |
 Employment      Plant               Sales           Accounts
                 Operations
     |               |                   |               |
 Industrial      Engineering &       Service         Audit
 Relations       Maintenance
     |               |                   |
 Employee        Quality Control     Physical
 Services                            Distribution
                     |                   |
                 Research            Overseas
```

**Figure 1. The Organization Structure
Madras Subsidiary of Fina Glassware Corporation.**

Ram Gopal was a devout Hindu, born into a Brahmin family. In the Indian caste system, the Brahmins are classified as the priestly class, a very orthodox group. Whether in making a major decision like fixing a date for wedding or performing a minor activity such as going out for some purpose, the time of the day and the day itself are very important to Brahmins. Ram Gopal would not undertake any activity which falls in the bad time of the day. He would rather postpone it, however important it was. From his birth to the present day, he had lived according to this system and never questioned it.

Ram joined Fina Glassware seven years ago after his Bachelor's degree in Technology from a local university. On a part-time basis, he completed his Diploma in Business Management. After working for three years in the Manufacturing department as a process engineer, he moved to the Marketing Department. Due to his accomplishments by exceeding marketing targets consistently, he was promoted to the position of marketing manager. He was modest, citing luck and the choice of time (the good time) as the reasons for his success.

All along, Ram had subordinates and bosses who were locals and who understood Ram's reasons for postponing decisions to suit the good time and good day. Now, Ram in his managerial position had to report directly to an expatriate manager from the United States who had an entirely different set of values.

Ram was in a dilemma. He had to produce the report by 2 pm but he was certain deep in his heart that the plan would not succeed if he laid the foundation for it in the 'bad time' of the day. He called George's secretary to try to postpone the two o'clock meeting to 4.30 pm. However, he was told by the secretary that George was out of the factory and would go straight to the meeting after his return.

As Ram sat motionless in his office, one of his sales executives, Charles Nathan, came to see him for a personal request. Since Charles was a Christian and did not go by the auspicious time and day, Ram asked him to compile some data for his report by 1.30 pm so that he could at least have something on paper for the 2.00 pm meeting with George. Charles took up the assignment gladly since his personal request was granted. He submitted the data in a series of tables and graphs to Ram at 1.30 pm. By the time Ram left for meeting, he had about 60% of the outline of the plan completed. He entered George's office:

Good Time and Bad Time at Fina Glassware

George   Hello! Ram. How are you? I am glad you were able to make it to the meeting.

Ram: Yes, Mr. Foster, but . . .

George: Let us sit down and have a chat before the others get in. By the way, let me glance through your outline.

Ram: (Handed over the report)

George: (As he glanced through it, he felt that the data was assembled in a haphazard manner and the report was not complete. His face turned red) Ram, I don't think we can go ahead with the meeting with what you have prepared. What happened to you? I was told that you are one of our best managers. Is it the kind of work you do? If you don't feel well, you better take a day off and go home and rest. Let some capable person do the job.

(George called his secretary and instructed her to inform the other participants of the meeting that it would not be held because Ram Gopal had not completed his report).

Ram: Mr. Foster! You see, when I came into your office this morning, I didn't realize that the time between 10.30 am and 1.30 pm was not auspicious for me to start this report. I have always chosen the most auspicious time to make my decisions and do important assignments.

George: What? We don't run things here according to good and bad times! In my view, all times are good. It depends on how we make use of it. If we are going to rely on good and bad times, it will lead to total inefficiency. You are paid for eight hours of work per day, not according to good and bad times.

Ram: Mr. Foster! Please look at my past accomplishments. All of them have been successful because I chose the auspicious time to do them!

George ended the discussion and told Ram to see him the next morning with the report. As Ram left, he felt that this was going to be a black mark in his performance. George, trained in the Western world, valued time as money. He could not understand the rationale for Ram's belief in good and bad time. His dilemma was whether to reprimand Ram for his negligence; or to forgive him and in future insist on his own value systems; or to adapt to the local values.

Meanwhile, he asked his secretary to place an order for a book on local customs and traditions.

11

The Progressive Hoe

Elena was jubilant. As she watched the hoes being packed into boxes on the factory floor, she felt a great sense of accomplishment. This was the first batch of "progressive" hoes produced by Progressive Farm Tools in Tanzania.

Six years ago, Elena started work with the Progressive Farm Machines Limited Company in the United States. The company now had a factory in Myeba which was in the Southern Highlands of Tanzania. Elena was in charge of marketing the farm tools produced by the Tanzanian factory.

There was a vast market for farming tools in Tanzania. Of Tanzania's population of 24 million, 90% lived in rural areas, depending on agriculture for their livelihood. Most of the Tanzanian farmers used rather backward farming methods and tools. In Tanzania, farming was the whole family's business. Most of the work on the farms was done by women and children. The men therefore regarded their wives and children as sources of income. Polygamy was seen as something desirable, so was having a large number of children.

The Tanzanian government had tried to encourage the modernization of agricultural practices by urging the farmers to use tractors, mechanical ploughs, better seeds and modern fertilizers. In line with its efforts, the government had invited Progressive Farm Machines to establish a factory in Tanzania. Progressive Farm

Machines was famous in the United States for its sophisticated farming equipment and machinery. Thus, when it received the invitation to open a factory in Tanzania and cater to the Tanzanian market, Progressive Farm Machines reacted with surprise.

There was discussion and debate among the managers of Progressive Farm Machines. Finally, they decided that it would be viable to open a factory in Tanzania. The huge Tanzanian market seemed attractive. The Tanzanian government's campaign to encourage the farmers to modernize would also make it easier for Progressive Farm Machines to sell its products. Moreover, the Tanzanian government had also pledged to help the factory import raw materials.

The management of Progressive Farm Machines held several meetings with representatives of all departments to discuss the Tanzanian government's invitation. Elena represented the Marketing department. The meetings, she now recalled, had been fraught with conflict and disagreement. The representatives of five departments (out of eleven) had been dead against opening a factory in Tanzania.

The opposing representatives had their reasons. They argued that Progressive Farm Machines had been producing advanced machinery and should continue to do so. To manufacture simple farm tools would not be in line with corporate strategy; it would be retrogressive and not progressive. Moreover, the tools would be "out of sync" with the company's name. Another representative had argued that the Tanzanian farmers would not buy Progressive's Products: "Our stuff won't sell. The peasants won't be able to afford our equipment. Do you want to operate at a loss?"

Elena had been, and still was convinced that the Tanzanian factory was a good idea. She firmly believed that opportunities should be exploited. During the meetings, she had pleaded for openness to the needs of the huge Tanzanian market. The representatives could not agree and finally, the decision was put to a vote. The result was six-four, with one abstention, in favor of opening a Tanzanian factory.

Progressive vs Traditional

Progressive Farm Machines had decided that its Tanzanian factory would, for a start, produce simple farming implements and improved versions of traditional farming tools. In line with this decision, the Tanzanian factory would be called "Progressive Farm Tools" and not "Progressive Farm Machines". The Design department was made

The Progressive Hoe

responsible for studying the traditional tools and suggesting new designs for them.

One of the most widely used farm tools in Tanzania was the hoe. The traditional hoe had been used by the Tanzanian farmers for centuries. Tanzanian farmers knew the traditional hoe by two brand names — "Rungwe" and "Crocodile". The traditional hoe had a thick, long and heavy handle. The blade was wider where it joined the handle and narrower at the edge. This is what it looked like:

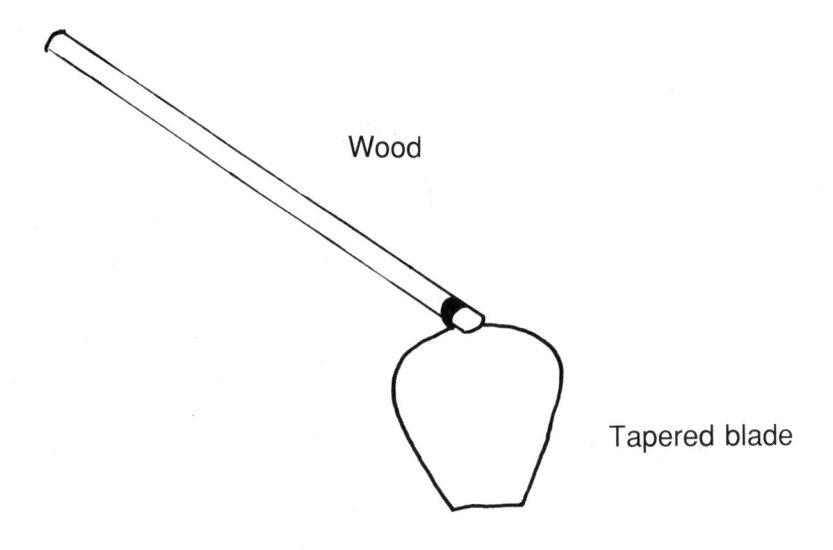

Figure 1. The Traditional Hoe

The Design department of Progressive Farm Tools was proud of its improved hoe. The progressive hoe, as it came to be called, had a thinner and lighter handle. The blade had the same width from top to bottom. It also had a smaller total area than the traditional blade. The blade was made of the steel. Figure 2 shows a sketch of the progressive hoe.

The Design department was confident that the Tanzanian farmers would prefer the progressive hoe. Not only was it lighter and stronger than the traditional hoe; it was also less bulky.

Culture and Management: A Casebook

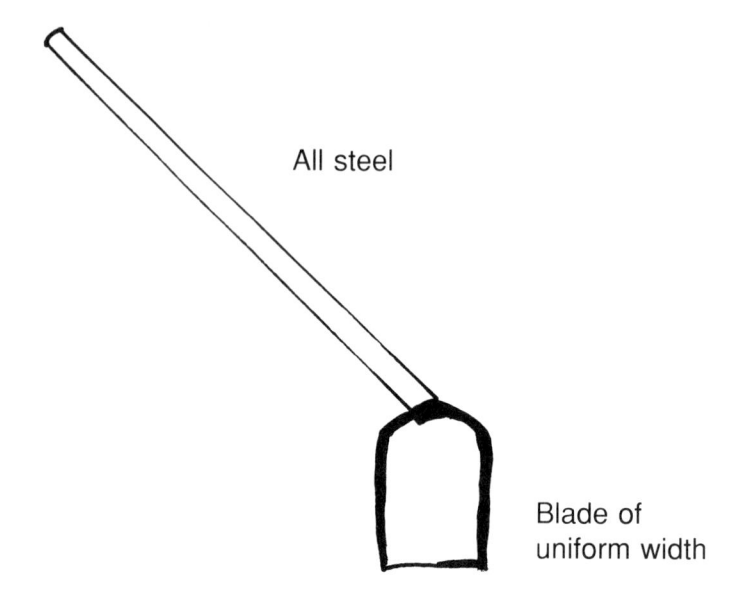

Figure 2. The Progressive Hoe (All steel; Blade of uniform width)

Elena and her colleagues in the Marketing department were delighted that the progressive hoe was going to be competitively priced — it would have the same price as the traditional hoe. Moreover, the farmers were facing a shortage of traditional hoes. Elena expected the progressive hoe to be a hit. "They just have to buy it," she enthused, "It's so elegant and progressive!".

The Outcome

In its first two months in the Tanzanian market, the progressive hoe did not sell well. Although some farmers did buy the hoe, the majority — an estimated 95% of the market — persistently refused to buy the progressive hoe.

The Tanzanian government redoubled its "Modernize Agriculture" campaign but was barely effective. As head of the Marketing department in Progressive's Tanzanian operations, Elena was terribly worried. She could not understand why the progressive hoe met with such a cold reception. This did not augur well for other implements and tools which Progressive had specially produced for the Tanzanian market. Exasperated, she murmured to herself, "I can't fathom those farmers! Why aren't they buying what's good for them?"

12

Corporate Culture vs National Culture

A Little About the Country

Nigeria has more than a hundred ethnic groups and consequently, numerous different cultures. It has three major tribes, each with its own distinct values. The Yoruba tribe places value on education, respect for elders, filial piety and preference for male children. The Ibo tribe emphasizes deep respect for family members, favoritism toward family and expression through actions rather than words. The Hawa tribe attaches little importance to formal education. It places importance on wives and children; children are regarded as symbols of wealth. Although there are many different tribes in Nigeria, some values are common to most of the tribes. They are loyalty to family and identification with one's village and fellow villagers.

Bendel Steel Company

The Bendel Steel Company, in the Bendel State of Nigeria, was established by the Federal Government in 1978. The plant was to be run as a commercial organization but was subject to government intervention and directives.

The managers of the Bendel Steel Plant were recruited by the government. Only well-qualified, experienced managers were recruited. Some of the managers were non-Nigerian; there were French, Dutch, Singaporean and even Japanese managers in the Bendel Steel Plant.

All the Nigerian managers had either received some formal education in a foreign country or had worked in another country besides Nigeria. The government hoped that by recruiting a group of managers with diverse exposure and experience, there would be more creativity and fresh ideas on how to run the Bendel Plant.

The government envisaged that the Bendel Steel Company would provide employment for a thousand Nigerians. Many jobs were available ranging from administrative, secretarial and clerical to those for engineers, technicians, machine operators and janitors.

Frank, the head of the Human Resource Division, was given the task of recruiting staff for the plant. Frank was a Nigerian who had a Bachelor's degree in Engineering from Scotland and a Master's degree in Business from the University of Michigan in the United States. Frank started his career as an Engineer in the United Kingdom, then became interested in management of personnel and industrial relations. After his Master's degree, he worked for several years in the United States holding various jobs of personnel manager, industrial relations manager and training manager. At the age of 40, he was invited by the Nigerian government to manage the Human Resource Division of the Bendel Steel Company. Thinking that it was time to return home and contribute more directly to his country, Frank accepted the invitation.

The Bendel Philosophy

The general manager of the Bendel Steel Company was Sam. Sam believed that the plant should have a philosophy to guide all employees. After a successful brainstorming session, Sam, Frank and the other senior managers formulated the Bendel philosophy and it included these four ideas:

1. Non-discrimination and non-favoritism (*Aisojusaju*). The managers considered *Aisojusaju* the key value of the Bendel Steel Company. They believed that to promote unity among the company's employees, the national value of favortism had to be countered. *Aisojusaju* was to guide all the company's policies and practices.
2. Equal opportunities for all employees to receive training, benefits and gain promotion, regardless of race, religion or tribe.
3. Commitment to hard work, innovation and co-operation.
4. Conformity to the highest ethical standards of truth, honesty and fairness, and respect for the rights of all employees.

Frank's Task

As Head of the Human Resources Division, Frank had to ensure that the Bendel philosophy would be translated into human resource practices. His first job was to recruit the numerous staff which the company needed. In all its advertisements for staff, the Bendel Steel company publicized its philosophy of *Aisojusaju*. Staff were selected according to the Bendel policy of recruiting the most able and well-qualified, regardless of their race, religion or tribe. Employees also had to have some sympathy for, if not belief, in the Bendel philosophy.

The result of the recruitment effort was that there was an uneven representation of tribes among the Bendel employees. The tribes which valued education, achievement and industry had a larger representation among the professional and executive staff. Some staff were recruited from other countries. Bendel Steel Company thus had a cosmopolitan mix of adventurous Korean, Indian, Australian, American and British employees.

Because the company had such a hodgepodge of employees, Frank and the other managers had to work hard to build unity.

The employees were recruited in groups. Each group of employees was made to attend a formal program of socialization. Each program was led by several senior managers. There were speeches, role-plays, workshops, discussions and sharings by both managers and employees. A critical outsider observing the program might be tempted to call it indoctrination or brainwashing. Nevertheless, the initiation of employees into the Bendel culture — its philosophy, practices and ways of doing things — was successful. Except for a few people who resigned because they could not identify with the Bendel culture, all the employees were happy to work for a company which stressed non-discrimination.

Frank and the managers were delighted. In the next few years, the Bendel Steel Company improved its performance and profits slowly but steadily. The Bendel Culture thrived, and some Nigerians praised it for its progressive values and outlook.

Sojusaju

In 1986, the Federal government tried to help its more backward, disadvantaged citizens. As part of its attempt to aid the disadvantaged states, the Federal government ordered its companies to give their

Corporate Culture vs National Culture

workforces "Federal Character". This meant that the companies had to employ people from all the 21 states and distribute posts of all levels to them.

The Federal government's effort upset Frank and the other managers very much. Clearly, *Aisojusaju* was being threatened and a form of *Sojusaju* (discrimination, in this case according to state) was being encouraged. Recruitment, rewards and promotion would no longer be given according to performance. In the long run, productivity and profits might fall. Frank felt particularly troubled because he was the human resource manager. If he did not abide by the government's directive, he would probably lose his job. But he could not simply change *Aisojusaju* human resource practices to *Sojusaju* ones. Besides, the employees, who had come to believe strongly in *Aisojusaju*, were protesting fiercely against the government's directive. The strongest protest came from employees who were due for promotion in a month's time. If the government's directive was obeyed, someone else from another state might be promoted instead. The expatriate staff also protested, partly because they did not agree with the directive and partly because their position in the company now seemed unclear.

The General Manager, Sam, was also torn between keeping the Bendel Culture and obeying the government. The other managers felt the same. Some managers even said that they would resign rather than obey. However, Frank could not bring himself to resign from the company. He knew that he should discharge his responsibilities as human resource manager. For him, it was a matter of honor to stay with the company during its crisis. A terrible conflict seemed to envelope his whole being. Frank personally believed in *Aisojusaju*, but now, he was forced to implement something which he did not believe in. He empathized with the employees but did not know how to help them. Just then, the telephone rang. The caller was Sam, who asked Frank to his office to discuss "this great misfortune".

13

Pedro's Cultural Maze

The Philippines

The Philippines, located between Australia and the South-east Asian countries of Singapore, Malaysia and Indonesia, is a group of islands. It is predominantly Christian; about 90% of the population is Christian. The country was under Spanish domination for over 350 years. The Americans dominated for 40 years while the Japanese occupied it for five years. All these dominations exerted influences on the people. Even today, these influences are reflected in the Filipino society. Yet, Filipinos still maintain some values of their own.

In Tagalog (a major Filipino language) *Hiya* means shame. In any social interaction, Filipinos are always careful not to "lose face". They tend to be tactful, diplomatic and careful not to offend anyone. Thus, confrontations are rare because "you do not tell one's faults straight to his face".

The literal translation for *Utang Naloob* is gratitude. The sense of gratitude or the feeling that one has to return a good deed or favor done for one, is an important cultural value. It makes people feel obliged to repay any good done for them. Failure to do so makes them an outcast and such people are regarded as someone who does not have *Utang Naloob*.

The Filipinos' faith in God is reflected in their cultural value of *Bahala Na*, which means "leave it to God (*Bahala* is God)." In the western view, this may be considered a fatalistic attitude. People adopt this attitude especially in times of crisis. When confronted with a problem, some Filipinos tend to avoid or ignore the seriousness of it by saying, *Bahala Na*, God will take care of it somehow.

Kagon is a kind of grass commonly found during summer months in Philippines. This grass covers vast fields and when it burns, a bright and brick-colored flame is emitted. The fire spreads quickly. However, it lasts only a short while. The cultural value of *Ningas Kagon* (*Kagon-fire*) reflects this. The Filipinos have a tendency to be enthusiastic about anything (a cause, fashion, etc.) with a burning passion which lasts only for a short while. Many social scientists say that this tendency has a negative impact on development, especially economic development, because the interest of people cannot be sustained and maintained in long-term industrial projects. Projects are started enthusiastically and when the interest is lost, they are either abandoned or simply terminated.

Batik

Mr Renkins, a Dutch entrepreneur, visited some Asian countries with the aim of exploring business venture opportunities. While visiting Indonesia, Malaysia and the Philippines, he was very much attracted to the *batik* cloth products in these countries. He thought that such material would have a good market potential not only in Holland but also in other European countries. He carried out a brief survey in his home country to determine the design, color and the quality preferences of consumers. Meanwhile, he conducted feasibility studies in Indonesia, Malaysia and the Philippines to set up a small factory to manufacture dyes necessary for the *batik* textiles, printing, and making a few clothing items initially.

The feasibility studies indicated that Philippines might be a better place for this business venture, given the availability of manpower, labor costs and natural dyes. During his previous trips to Philippines, Renkins had established good relations with some government officials and small businessmen. He thought that such contacts would be handy if decided to set up a business venture in Philippines. Further, since most of the Filipinos spoke or understood English, Renkins thought that communication would not be a problem. He was also impressed by the pleasant manners and temperaments of the Filipinos. All these strengthened his decision to set up a factory in Philippines. Although he had visited the Philippines on three or four occasions, he was not very familiar with the cultural values of Filipinos. He had only superficial knowledge of the country and its people.

Given his busy schedule and other business commitments elsewhere, Renkins could not work permanently in the Philippines. So, after interviewing several candidates for the job of factory manager, Renkins offered the job to Pedro, who was in his mid-forties and had a Bachelor's degree in Science and some business experience in the manufacturing industry. The factory started to function with an employee strength of about 50. Pedro was in charge of all aspects of factory operations including personnel, finance and general administration. He was well-versed with local conditions and problems. The factory started to function smoothly after the initial teething problems were taken care of.

Renkins was present for the factory opening but returned to Holland once the teething problems were solved. However, he kept in close touch with Pedro through telephone, telex and fax services. Initially, it appeared that everything was moving according to expectation. Employees were cooperative and enthusiastic about their work. Soon, however, the *Ningas-Kogan* effect crept in among the employees. Employees slowly started to demonstrate a careless attitude, resulting in quality, delay and other problems.

On one occasion an employee accidentally made a mistake in the mixing of the raw materials for the preparation of dyes for the *batik* material. Instead of reporting the matter to his supervisor, he just prayed that the mistake would not cause much difficulty. This type of attitude made it difficult for supervisors to implement stricter quality control measures, which are critical for exporting a product, especially to European countries.

Pedro was concerned about these problems although they were rectified from time to time. He thought that time was needed to bring these problems under control. Therefore, he decided not to convey these incidents to Renkins who was under the impression that everything was moving smoothly under the able leadership of Pedro.

Renkins slowly learnt that shipments from Philippines lagged behind schedules. But he did not press Pedro the reasons for delay. He thought that he would give them some time to shape up. Anyhow, he sent a mild reminder to Pedro. Upon receiving the message, Pedro was worried and feared that if he failed to meet schedules, he might lose his newly-found job. If he were sacked from this job, getting another job might prove difficult.

After analyzing the situation, Pedro found that much of the delay was caused by a particular supervisor, Ilano, in the dye-mixing department. Ilano was having problems with his own workers. Since the initial enthusiasm was slowly fading among the workers, he found it difficult to motivate them to keep up with deadlines and quality standards. While Pedro felt uncomfortable about communicating his message to Ilano, it was difficult for Ilano to pass on the message to his workers. The Filipino cultural value of *Hiya* ("Face") stood as a barrier and no immediate action could be taken to remedy the situation. In situations of this sort, most often than not, the supervisor or manager would not directly reprimand a particular subordinate for his shortcomings and failures. Instead they would tell another subordinate who happens to be a friend of that subordinate about the problem so that he or she could pass on the message. The manager then waits to see if some action follows. Thus the peer-level communication is preferred to supervisor-subordinate communication when it comes to passing on the unpleasant messages in work situations. Direct confrontation is avoided because the subordinate should not "lose face". If the faults are not that serious and can be remedied or if the offenses are just first-time ones, then supervisors can communicate those messages in a more positive tone, saying, "Next time, please try to improve". When peer-level communication takes place, people tend to receive the suggestion without "loss of face" and may even make a better attempt to change or improve.

Pedro's predicament was getting greater and greater as the pressure of time was building on him. He was accountable to Renkins and soon might have to report the situation to him. Renkins might not understand and appreciate this particular cultural value of Filipinos. If he did not inform and seek advice from Renkins, he might prolong the problem, aggravating it and causing more damage. That would lead him to lose his job. But, if he did convey news about the state of affairs — the delays in meeting deadlines and the cultural problems he was facing — it would indicate his inefficiency and poor leadership qualities. He almost came close to making a phone call to Renkins but abandoned the idea and asked the secretary to cancel the call. He gathered enough courage to face up to the situation and decided to talk to Ilano about his shortcomings. Pedro could not afford to take a *Bahala Na* attitude.

Pedro had to think very carefully about how to deal with this situation without really offending Ilano, yet at the same time getting the message across to him. In fact Pedro had a cordial, friendly relationship with Ilano. Once he was invited to Ilano's house for a special celebration. He was treated very well by the family and was given a few gifts to take home. While contemplating his course of action, Pedro was reminded of all these past incidents and the cultural value of *Utang Na Loob*, (showing gratitude for one's kindness). If he were to reprimand Ilano, that might be construed as an unkind act by Ilano and other employees in the factory. During his visit to Ilano's house, Ilano's parents requested Pedro to take good care of their son.

Pedro was under severe cultural constraints. He had to respond to a series of questions in formulating a solution which would enhance his image, help to maintain good relations with his employees and enable him to keep his job. The questions in his mind were: How can I sustain the enthusiasm of the employees and prevent them from succumbing to the cultural value of *Ningas Kogan* (*Kogan-Fire*)? How can I enforce quality standards so vital to export business and not leaving everything to God (*Bahala Na*)? How can I overcome the cultural value of *Hiya* (shame) and yet take prompt actions when necessary? Specifically, how can I give the message directly to Ilano to shape up or leave the company? How can I help Ilano to pass on the same message to his subordinates?

Pedro left his office on Friday evening, planning to find answers to these questions during the weekend.

14

Goertz's Experience In Thailand

Thailand is one of the few countries in South-east Asia which has never succumbed to any kind of colonial rule. It is, however, surrounded by countries such as India, Burma, Malaysia, Cambodia, Vietnam and Singapore which were colonized until recent times. Some Thais ascribe Thailand's modern day problems to the fact that it has never been colonized, while other Thais are proud that Thailand has always been a sovereign state.

The Thais have preserved many of their traditional values. They are extremely polite, warm, kind and show a great deal of tolerance. But they become emotional and lose their balance when driven to intolerable situations. Any amount of criticism, if given privately, will be accepted. But if such criticism is given in public, the receiver's rage will know no bounds. After witnessing the politeness of Thai people, it would be a frightening experience to observe them when they are emotionally upset.

It is said that Thai people think more for themselves and their own welfare rather than that of their company or society. Under these conditions, it may not be realistic for organizations to seek absolute loyalty from employees.

The expatriate executive may find it hard to ascertain the views of Thai employees because they do not express them. Expression of one's opinions in public might be considered impolite. In meetings, discussions and work group sessions where superiors are present, it is difficult to get them involved in discussions. Participative management is hindered and such behavior may pose a problem in building work groups and teams.

Slowness in getting things done is also an accepted practice in Thailand. It is said that the Thais work half the speed of the Japanese. Haste does not make sense to them. Time is treated in a cyclical way, if the time goes, it will come again. *Mei Pen Rai* (never mind) and *Astha Maniana* (for everything there is tomorrow) are common sayings.

The Thai employees prefer to follow orders very closely. In doing so, however, they risk losing the power to think independently, initiate and execute plans. An average Thai accepts change quickly at the individual level, for instance, changes in fashion or at the political level such as changes of government.

It is important for expatriate executives who wish to effectively manage employees in Thailand to look beyond the "nice smile" of the Thai people and try to understand their value systems.

This case describes the experience of a Swiss executive who was posted to his company's subsidiary in Thailand. The headquarters of this subsidiary is in Bangkok. The subsidiary markets pharmaceutical and agricultural products in Thailand. The subsidiary also manufactures products at its Thai plant.

Goertz

After serving three years in the Netherlands subsidiary of ABIC Pharamaceutical Company, Mr Goertz was posted to Thailand as Product Manager — Dyestuffs and Chemicals Division. This was his first assignment in Asia. His Asian exposure was limited to one or two conference attendances in the past. He was enthusiastic in accepting his new assignment. He was provided with excellent benefits such as, housing, company car with chauffeur and a maid to help with the household chores. Since all these personal problems were taken care of, Goertz found it easy to adjust to living in Thailand and to his day-to-day work.

A week after settling in the job, he met the regional manager to keep him informed of the Division's progress. When the regional manager asked him how he liked his new home and the new job, Goertz replied "Oh, I like this place very much. The people are nice and polite. I don't think I will have any problems in doing my job. If

Goertz's Experience in Thailand

I need any assistance, I know where to go." The regional manager then wished him good luck and told him that he would be on his own from now on.

Goertz took time to get to know his office staff which consisted of six managers, 20 supervisors, a dozen clerical staff and secretaries. After getting to know their names and designations, Goertz felt better and thought he could get on with the work.

Goertz wanted to get more information about the ABIC products which were packaged and marketed in Thailand. He set up a schedule to meet each manager individually to discuss matters pertaining to that manager's product area. Suntivong was the first one to meet Goertz. He had been an employee of the company for eight years and was senior to many other managers in the subsidiary. This is their conversation:

Goertz: Hello, come on in Mr Suntivong! How are you?
Suntivong: Thank you, Sir. I am fine with your blessings.
Goertz: I heard you are the senior person in our division and you have been with the company for over eight years or so. Am I right?
Suntivong: You are right, Sir! I like this company very much.
Goertz: I need some briefing from you as to how some of our dyestuffs are doing and what your thoughts are on improving the market coverage for those items. Can you do this soon, say, by next week?
Suntivong: I shall be pleased to do so, Sir. I will get the information for you.

A week later, Goertz asked Suntivong for the requested information and told him to be ready for a briefing. But Suntivong did not take the request seriously. Just to be polite, he told him in his first meeting that he would get the information. Goertz was anxiously hoping to have briefing from Suntivong. Instead, Suntivong told him that he would collect all the information in a short while and brief him then. Goertz was a little disappointed. But without expressing his disappointment explicitly, he told Suntivong to get the information soon.

The first weekly management meeting was scheduled a few days after Goertz met Suntivong. Some issues were discussed during the meeting and after the agenda of the meeting was completed, Goertz asked Suntivong whether he had completed his assignment and was ready to have a discussion with him after the meeting. When he heard Suntivong say "I will do it soon, Sir," he became furious and his face turned red. The managers could see his reaction to Suntivong's response. Goertz turned to Suntivong and told him, "I can't understand a Senior Manager like you coming out with all sorts of excuses and not doing your job promptly. I can't and will not tolerate this type of attitude." Suntivong was embarrassed to have received such a reprimand in front of his colleagues and became emotional. His voice quaking, he told Goertz, "You foreigners come to our country and want everything handed over nicely and quickly. You don't know our problems. You don't understand our culture." With these words, Suntivong left the conference room.

Goertz returned to his office and tried to calm himself. He knew he had made a *faux pas*. He was trying to analyze where he went wrong. He remembered his predecessor telling him that "when you give instructions to employees, be clear and precise. When an assignment is made, confirmation or checking is needed to see whether they understood the assignment. If you happened to criticize or reprimand them, do it privately. The Thai may be easy going but he or she can be made more productive if Thai nature is well understood."

As Goertz went home, he narrated his experience at work to his wife. His wife was sympathetic but could not help him with an answer. Instead, she handed him a small paperback book on Thai culture. She told him to glance through it while she was preparing the dinner. By next morning, he must have an answer whether to reconcile with Suntivong or take some tough measures to introduce certain standards as he had done in the Netherlands. He would need some assistance in coping with "foreign" situations in the future.

15

Mechanization At The Ethiopian Postal Service

Ethiopia

Ethiopia is a multi-cultural country located in the Eastern part of Africa. It has a population of 43 million. More than 70 languages are spoken throughout the country. One may not be able to identify a typical Ethiopian culture because of the diversity in living habits, values, beliefs, religious background and languages. Administrators in the public sector and managers in the private sector often find it difficult to close the sub-cultural gaps and create harmony among people from various sub-cultures. At times, these administrators and managers have to exercise a greater degree of flexibility in dealing with problems.

Apart from cultural problems, there are some internal and external factors in organizations which impede the effective practice of management. For instance, the highly centralized planning system introduced by the socialist government since 1978 does not leave much room for administrators to use a contingency approach to management. Frequent and often unnecessary interventions by the government officials, union representatives and party officials make it difficult to be efficient and effective, thus productivity is limited. The major losers in this type of environment are the public-sector organizations. The case presented here is of one such organization — the Ethiopian Postal Service.

The Ethiopian Postal Service (EPS)

The Ethiopian Postal Service is considerably a large public enterprise with 1500 employees and 400 branch post offices throughout the country. The administrators of the Postal Service, who have risen through the ranks, have little or no exposure to modern management techniques and practices. The Postal Service may be described as antiquated. Most of the top and middle level administrators in the Postal Service have been in the same jobs for at least 15 years or so. Due to employees' resistance to new ideas and changes, the Postal Service could not introduce some modern systems and procedures. Added to this, automation was not in line with the socialist government's idealogy.

By the end of 1982, there were five big air and surface mail exchange offices in different parts of the country. The volume of mail had increased at a constant rate over the years. The famine in Ethiopia drew the attention of the world and aid flowed in from different parts of the world in parcels and packages. Even with the automation and modern facilities, postal services in developed countries have in recent years found it difficult to handle ever-increasing volumes of mail. One can well imagine the difficulty of sorting and delivering mail in Ethiopia where the infrastructure is poor. There are few transportation and communication linkages and villages are scattered throughout the country.

Assab Exchange Office

Assab Exchange Office is one of the biggest Exchanges in the country. The exchange could not handle the increasing volume of mail due to limited building facilities, equipment and manpower. The work at the Exchange almost came to a standstill. There was a large number of complaints from various quarters about loss of mail or delay in delivery.

Realizing the pressures and problems, the administrators of the Exchange made the following proposals:

Construct a bigger building and increase the number of employees
or
Mechanize the monotonous and repetitive operational functions.

The proposals were presented to the Minister for Communications for his guidance and approval. Both proposals

Mechanization at the Ethiopian Postal Service

required quite a big investment. The first proposal was rejected, the reason being the high cost of construction in the Assab port area. Assab has extremely high temperatures averaging 40 to 42 degrees centigrade. It would also be very costly to transport building materials to Assab.

Given the high cost of the first proposal, the second alternative seemed more feasible. Mechanization offered the benefits of lower operational costs. It was expected to reduce labor requirements, improve efficiency and enhance working conditions. Despite protests from the universal postal union and its local counterpart, the Minister for Communications approved the second alternative with some minor modifications.

Mechanization

In the first phase, measures were taken to identify the necessary equipment and machinery. A task force was formed to identify the equipment and install it. The task force visited some of the neighboring African and East European countries to study the installation methods and problems associated with mechanization. Upon the recommendations of the task force, the equipment was installed in the Assab Exchange Office. Thus the second phase of the project was completed. In the third phase, the employees were given training in operating the system and functioning in the new work environment. Then they were put on the job and further training was given. Not everything went according to plan. During the period of training, certain problems were discovered. They had been overlooked during the planning stage.

The Cultural Factor

Assab city and its surroundings are not conducive to work because of the hot climate. Not many professionals would want to work in this area. *Afar* is the only tribe which is accustomed to living in this area. People in this area usually work only in the mornings. In the afternoon, groups of five or six people form social gatherings which are called *Bercha*. The *Bercha* members then make conversation and eat the leaves of a particular plant, known as *Ghat* which has a stimulating effect.

During these gatherings, people sit on the floor in a circular form and discuss issues for hours and hours until night. People are thus accustomed to sitting on the floor. Chairs are a rarity in houses in the Assab area. Instead, big mattresses are used. This habit of sitting on the floor was carried over to workplaces too. In the Assab Post Office, employees used to sit on the floor while sorting mail. They were not used to sitting on chairs for long hours.

It might be prudent to state here that the *Bercha Group* social activities practised in the Assab area do not necessarily lead to negative effects. In some organizations, such groups are used for solving work-related problems. It is the belief of Assab people that the stimulating effect of the *Ghat* leaf boosts creativity and increases the levels of thinking and concentration. However, there is as yet no scientific research to prove this claim.

After mechanization, the layout of the Assab Post Office was completely changed. Chairs were fixed around the sorting machine and the conveyor belt. The trainees were asked to perform their jobs while sitting on the chairs. However, they could not get used to the new ways of doing things. The employees were not told or convinced of the change. Thus, the new situation posed a potential conflict between the employees and the administration.

The employees who could not adapt to the situation slowly walked out of their jobs. Working in the Post Office was no longer a pleasure for them. On the contrary, it was rather painful to have to sit on those chairs while carrying on with their activities. In order to cope with the problem of high turnover, the Chief of Postal Service decided to transfer some employees from post offices in other regions to Assab city. This increased the cost of operation. The initial expectation of higher productivity, speed and decreased costs could not be realized. The situation prior to the installation of mechanization appeared to be far better. Although there were delays and complaints before the mechanization, the employees seemed happier and relations among them were much friendlier.

At the Assab Post Office, the postal operations almost came to a standstill. The administrators were caught in a dilemma. On the one hand, they had to make the system work or face the wrath of the government authorities. Soon they might have to go to the Minister for Communications and tell him about the failure of the new system. On the other hand, they had a trying time training the employees to adapt to the new system and keeping them in the organization. They were also running out of time.

16

Blood Is Thicker Than Water

Zambia and Its Tribes

Zambia is an African country noted for its diversity of cultural beliefs, values and tribal groups. About 72 different dialects are spoken by the people belonging to different tribal groups. Each tribal group has its own unique value system reflected in a behavior typical of that tribe.

The seven main tribes of Zambia are the Lozi, Bemba, Ngoni, Tonga, Luvale, Kaonde and Lunda. These tribes are further sub-divided according to the dialect spoken. The Lozi tribe, also known as Aluyanas, occupies the Western part of Zambia. The word *Aluyan* means "people of the plains and waters". Some of the sub-groups of Lozi tribe are Subuya, Toka, Nkoya, Nyengo, Alogi and Mukwamakomas.

The Bemba tribe occupies the Northern part and the Copper Belt of Zambia. The sub-groups, based on the dialects spoken by this group, are Bisa, Namwanga and Lala. The Ngoni tribe, also commonly known as Nyanja, is concentrated in the Eastern part of Zambia and extends to the neighboring Malawi. Chewa, Tambulla and Senga are the sub-groups of this tribe. The earliest settlers of Zambia come from the Tonga tribe who live in the southern part of the country. They are traditionally farmers. The sub-tribal groups include the Tokaleya, Govas and Ilas. The Luvale, Kaonde and Lunda tribes are found in the North-western province of Zambia. These three tribes have similar customs and beliefs. It is believed that all of these tribes have come from the

Lunda-Luba Kingdom of Congo, another African country. Their subgroups include Chokwe, Luchazi and Mbunda.

The people belonging to various tribes believe in some form of supernatural power and call it by different names such as Mulimu, Lesa and Mulungu. All of them mean 'God'. But the description of this divine power varies from tribe to tribe. For instance, the people belonging to Lozi tribe believe that God had a wife and their kings and queens are descendants of this first family. Thus, the power of the Royal family becomes supreme because they are the descendants of God. The people from this tribe are very loyal not only to the members of the Royal family but to any leader who is inspired or has any association with God.

The close-knit solidarity which results from tribalism leads to nepotism and favoritism at all levels in society. Such ties become important criteria in the recruitment, selection, promotion of staff, and in other personnel decisions. Managers from a particular tribe are obliged to favor their own tribesmen regardless of the latter's capabilities and skills. Such practices create problems at the workplace – laziness, lack of initiative and loss of motivation. Managing people with these attitudes becomes difficult. Once they know that they have strong tribal ties, people, especially those belonging to influential families, no longer bother to work either to gain admission into schools and colleges, to gain employment or to get promoted.

The values of people from different tribes seem to reflect their placement in different types of industries and business organizations. For instance, the Lozis are known to be loyal and highly dedicated to work wherever they are placed. These values help them to find placement in banks, security firms, and in many technical jobs. On the other hand, some tribes do not find any value in education. This may be because over centuries, they were getting their livelihood from cattle and view children as helpers. Some tribes refuse to send their female children to school. With this attitude, it becomes difficult for females to find employment or to hold responsible positions.

Matale

John Matale, a bright young man from the Lozi tribe, was sent to the United Kingdom on a special scholarship to study Public Administration in a prestigious university. After learning the fundamentals, principles and techniques of effective Public Administration for two years, Matale returned to Zambia. He was posted to the Management Services Department in the Civil Service to receive on-the-job training under Sam Mawunde, an experienced civil servant who was due to retire in a year's time.

On his first day at work, Matale was briefed about the Civil Service, its prevailing culture and his job responsibilities. As part of his job, he was given the responsibilities of reviewing the systems and procedures.

A significant portion of Matale's job involved reviewing the existing systems and procedures, particularly those related to personnel practices and making recommendations to improve the system.

In order to acquaint himself with the Civil Service culture and existing practices, Matale drew up a schedule for his visits to Administration departments in various Ministries and government agencies. Equipped with his academic knowledge and enthusiasm, Matale started his assignment with high expectations although he was warned of certain obstacles by his superior. Restoring efficiency was his main concern.

As he was progressing with his visits and interviews with some selected people in various Ministries and agencies, he found that over 70% of non-technical and managerial positions in Zambian Civil Service were occupied by people from the Ngoni tribe. One of his administrative assistants reminded him of the common saying among the Ngonis, *Mwana ws kwatu* which means 'my blood relationship'. This saying is applied to anyone from the Eastern Province of Zambia, especially the Tumbukas, a sub-group of Ngonis. Matale felt that this belief probably led to nepotism and explained why the Civil Service was filled with Ngonis.

Matale was disturbed by the extent to which nepotism was rampant in the Civil Service. He wanted to get more insights into how nepotism influenced personnel decisions. He himself identified about a dozen people for his interview. These interviewees were from the Ngoni tribe as well as from other tribal groups.

Matale had an interesting session with Rick Kwono from the Engineering Services Division. Kwono was from the Bemba tribe which is in the Northern part of Zambia. Part of the interview is reported on the following page.

Culture and Management: A Casebook

Matale: How long have you been with the Engineering Services Division, Rick?
Kwono: For about eight years.
Matale: How do you like your job?
Kwono: The job is okay. But I can't stand the favoritism shown by my superiors and colleagues. Since most of them are Ngonis, they speak in their own dialect and expect you to learn their dialect. When there is a position available, they are the first to know about it. By the time you know it, the position is already filled by a Ngoni.
Matale: If favoritism is practised that widely, how, being a Bemba, did you get your job?
Kwono: You may call it 'Divine Providence' or luck. I was one of the four short-listed for the job. Of the rest, two were Ngonis and one Lozi. In terms of education and experience, I was better qualified than the rest. Two of the short-listed candidates (a Ngoni and the Lozi) pulled out to join businesses operated by their relatives. I was much better qualified than the Ngoni and it was difficult for the interviewers to go against me. They gave me the job and found another place for the other candidate.
Matale: What criteria do you think they use in recruitment and selection?
Kwono: I am not aware of any specific criteria being used in selection. If you look at the type of people we have here, you may come to a conclusion that 'whom you know' matters. You've got to have someone from your tribe to get a job.

Matale was depressed after the interview. He returned to his office and reflected on the culture that prevailed in the Civil Service. Nepotism seemed to be the guiding principle of all the personnel decisions. Since the time of independence in 1964 until the present, about 70% of the supervisory and managerial positions in the Civil Service had been monopolized by one tribe. In the government offices, the official language had become the language spoken by the people belonging to this tribe, the Ngoni. Being a member of this tribe automatically gave one the passport to a good position in the Civil Service.

Matale did not know where to start. On the one hand, he had to play safe since he was from a minority tribe and his position would be at stake. On the other hand, if he did not do a good job in making recommendations to improve the system and implement them, he might be considered incapable. Matale was in a dilemma.

17

The Lunar Seventh Month At Allied Service Industries

Allied Service Industries

Allied Service Industries (ASI) was a diversified group of companies in Hong Kong which specialized in automotive repair services. Though a large part of its business for repair services came from the military establishment, commercial vehicles are also serviced when schedules permit to do so. ASI is noted for its quality of service and it has computerized its services recently too.

The employees at ASI were highly disciplined. Customer satisfaction was high, and the turnover rate of employees was low. On its part, ASI made sustained efforts to increase employee productivity by introducing incentive schemes and improving the work environment. Among other things, the employees enjoyed subsidized meals, free uniforms and discounted rates for servicing their own vehicles.

ASI had six divisions — the heavy vehicles division, military trucks division, taxi service division, public sector commercial vehicles division, private vehicles division and an administrative unit. Foremen were in charge of the service divisions, each of which had approximately 15 to 20 mechanics and helpers. While the foreman was given the title "workshop controller", the employees reporting to him were given the title "service advisors". The salaries of service advisors varied considerably and depended on the advisors' length of service.

The annual performance review of the service advisors was

conducted by the workshop controller. Some key criteria for appraising performance included the ability to get along with fellow employees, discipline, job knowledge, willingness to work over time and cooperation. Generally, the advisors were happy with their annual ratings and the rewards and incentives which followed.

Charles

Charles Wong, one of the service advisors in the private vehicles division had worked in ASI for more than eight years. Soon after receiving his automotive engineering diploma from the Hong Kong Polytechnic, he joined ASI although he had four other job offers. While studying at the polytechnic, Charles had completed a part-time apprentice program at ASI. He was impressed by the work conditions and interpersonal relations at ASI. During his apprenticeship, Charles developed good relations with his boss, William Chong. His positive experience at ASI made Charles accept permanent employment with ASI after graduation.

Charles was 28 years old and well-built. He received high ratings in his recent physical fitness report. He had a very pleasant manner and socialized well with fellow employees. The younger employees considered him their big brother. He often spent his free time teaching the younger employees and helping them solve their problems. The workshop controller was fully aware of Charles's good deeds and quality workmanship. In all his eight years of service, Charles was rated 'outstanding' in his overall performance and thus received a handsome incentive award annually. No one in the division disputed his performance ratings.

Charles paid close attention to his customers' needs and meticulously completed their jobs. The customers developed a liking for Charles and often insisted that he should service their vehicles. Some of them sent letters of appreciation to his boss, commending Charles's courtesy and quality of workmanship.

Everything was going well for Charles and the concensus among his peers was that he should be groomed for promotion so that when the workshop controller retires in two years, Charles would take his place.

The employees were given two coffee breaks, one in the morning between 10.15 and 10.30 and a second one in the afternoon between 3.15 and 3.30. During the coffee breaks, the entire group of service advisors would sit together and talk about various topics such as films they had been to, movie stars, sports, games and other social activities. They would tease each other. The teasing was always taken light-heartedly, because interpersonal relations were good. Occasionally, the workshop controller also joined them.

The 15th day of the Lunar Seventh Month

One afternoon — on the 15th day of the Lunar Seventh month — Charles walked into the workshop. He smiled as he approached Lee, a junior mechanic. "Hi, Lee, how's work on that vehicle? Will it be ready by tomorrow?"

Lee had worked in ASI for two years. He reported to Charles. He had a high regard for Charles and always tried to oblige him even if it was inconvenient. Charles was like a big brother to him. At times he consulted Charles on his personal problems. Once, Lee had difficulty finding accommodation. Charles invited Lee to stay with him in his two-bedroom flat. Lee stayed at Charles's flat for ten days before finding his own accommodation.

Now, when Charles approached Lee about the client's vehicle, Lee replied that he was unaware of what work had been done on the vehicle. He added: "None of the others are around and I cannot do anything about it". Irritated by the response, Charles grabbed Lee by the collar and shouted expletive at him. Lee, ruffled, said, "Charles, don't get upset. Let's go outside and discuss the problem." That seemed to anger Charles all the more. He punched Lee several times before he was restrained by the other service advisors. Lee was silent and did not fight back. He only tried to defend himself and did little to provoke Charles.

The employees in the division were totally shaken by the incident. What happened did not match what they knew of Charles. Some of them had known Charles for more than six years. They respected him as a calm person who had a great deal of understanding and tolerance.

They also knew about the friendship between Charles and Lee. They all said, "This couldn't have happened".

Immediately after the incident, Lee lodged a written complaint to the Personnel department. ASI required strict discipline of its employees and would not tolerate any incidents of this sort. The policy in the area of discipline stated: "Anyone who engages in threatening behavior or physical violence within the premises will be dismissed."

The Lunar Seventh Month at Allied Service Industries

The workshop controller felt sorry for Charles. He tried to pacify Lee and persuade him to withdraw the complaint. Although Lee attempted to withdraw the complaint, the Personnel department refused to let him do so. The Personnel Manager abided by ASI's policy and dismissed Charles.

When asked why he lost his cool over such an apparently minor matter, Charles replied that he did not know what came over him and that he was not his normal self. One of the elderly service advisors quipped, "You should have known that it is the Lunar Seventh month and exercised more care at work".

Among the Chinese, the approach of the seventh month of the lunar year is traditionally viewed with trepidation. Street shows are held, festive offerings are made and incense is burned to appease the hungry souls who are supposedly released from the inner regions of hell on their autumn vacation. The workers at ASI had dutifully played their part to appease the "hungry ghosts" and the management had generally been tolerant of their offerings and activities in the ASI premises. This year, however, word got around that something was amiss. It was reported that in a single day, there was a record of two fights and a near-fight among the employees.

When the siren sounded at the end of the work day, the employees at Private Vehicles Department said that they should get together and have the Lunar Seventh month festivities or at least burn incense at the work premise before something more drastic happened.

Meanwhile, William Chong, the head of the Private Vehicles Department, was troubled by the fights. He sat in his office wondering how he should help Charles, one of his most diligent and trusted employees. After all, he reasoned, Charles was an innocent victim of the hungry ghosts of the Lunar Seventh month. William had to come out with some solutions for the following questions:

Should he accept the cultural explanation and end the matter? What else could have been the cause for the behavior of Charles who had an excellent work record? What options are left to resolve his dilemma?

18

Brazil's Too Far Away From Home

Sinlect

Sinlect is a Singapore company (incorporated in 1977) which is among the pioneers in high technology manufacturing in South East Asia. It grew rapidly and expanded its operations internationally. Its net earnings rose from S$250,000 in 1980 to its present figure of S$11.5 million. It started by employing 300 workers and now employs about 7,000 people worldwide.

Sinlect believes that its overseas factories should be managed only by Singaporeans of high calibre. There are a total of nine overseas factories; each managed by a Singaporean General Manager. By their natural geographical location, the factories are collectively overseen by their respective regional directors. These individuals are given full autonomy over their operations and, so far, this system has worked well. The selection of individuals to these appointments has always been stringent.

The Corporate Headquarters is located on the same premises as one of Sinlect's first two factories in Singapore. One of the reasons for Sinlect's success lies in its simple and yet extensive communication network. Its Marketing Division actively probes the external environment to sense changes in demand, competitor pricing and political milieu. Figure 1 shows the organization structure of Sinlect.

Except for a few, the managers of the company are relatively

Brazil's Too Far Away from Home

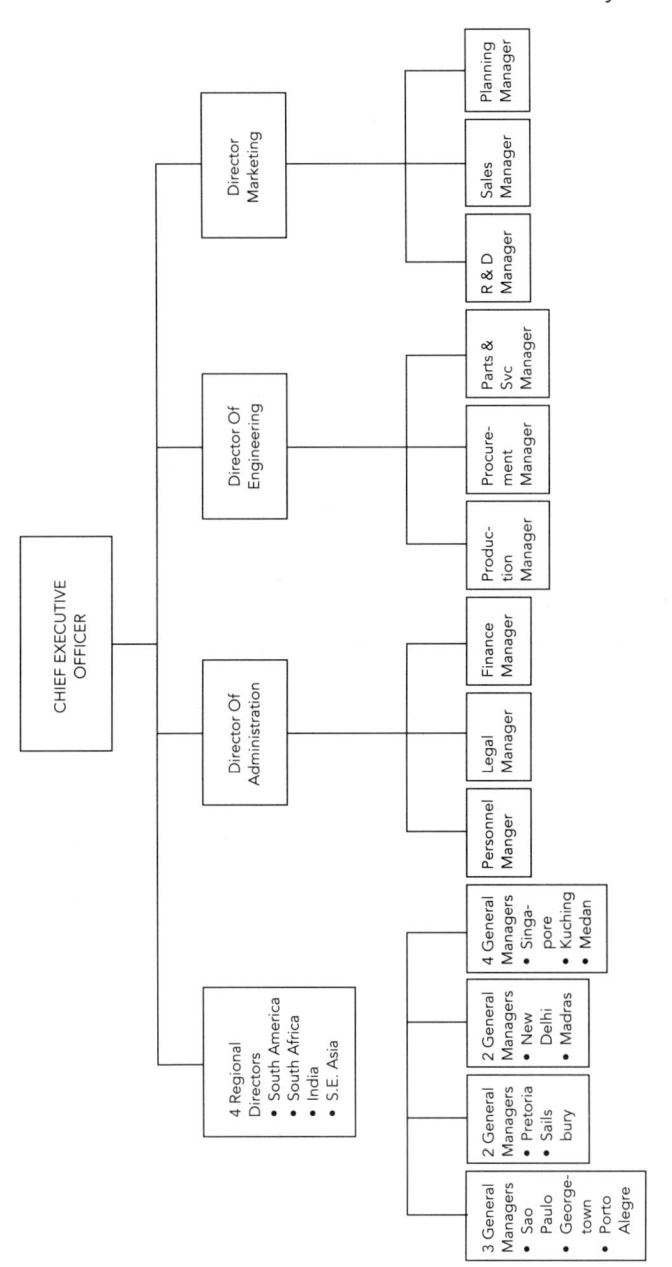

Fig. 1. The Organization Structure of Sinlect

young; most of them are in their mid-thirties. The Chief Executive Officer (CEO) is a former civil servant while the other managers were recruited from local and overseas universities. All the top managers are graduates in Electronic Engineering, a fact which emphasizes the technical nature of the business.

The company benefited from the management of two previous CEOs who were well recognized for their intelligence and humanism. The present CEO makes it his personal responsibility to visit the Regional Offices as often as time permits. However, he lacks skill in handling interpersonal relationships. This is a case about Paul Lim, the Chief Executive Officer, and one of his regional directors, Daniel Tsu.

In Brazil

Paul Lim, chief executive of Sinlect was whisked at high speed through the streets of Sao Paulo, the largest city in South America, and out to the villa of his regional director, Daniel Tsu.

He and Daniel had been in business meetings all day at the company's city-center offices and as this was a social occasion, Paul took along a box of truffles he had purchased in Paris for Daniel's wife, Michelle.

Before leaving for Sao Paulo, Paul had been warned by his Personnel Manager, Ronald Seah, that the Tsus were going through a difficult time. "She doesn't like Brazil very much and she positively hates Sao Paulo," Ronald had said, "although I can think of worse places to live. After all, it is more metropolitan than Singapore and there is no danger of being lonely."

Paul had learnt from Daniel himself that he had suggested that his wife return to Singapore to live with her parents for a while. But she had refused, saying she preferred to be unhappy alongside her husband than away from him. A mutual acquaintance had also told Paul that Michelle was intensely jealous of her husband and felt that his roving eye would turn to infidelity should she be packed off to Singapore for an indefinite period.

That night, dinner at the Tsu residence turned out to be quite embarrassing for Paul. Inevitably and very quickly, the conversation focussed on Singapore. Efforts by the Singapore Tourist Promotion Board to attract tourists from South America had increased the Tsu's consciousness that they were indeed far from home. Furthermore, they had learnt that the company had recently opened a new and luxurious headquarters on Orchard Road.

"Surely," Paul had said, "you have a lovely mansion, a circle of close friends, and you can go to the races just down the road. There are a lot of compensations — wouldn't you say so, Daniel?"

At this, Daniel's wife exploded. Normally cool and calm, she admonished Paul for trying to compare Sao Paulo with Singapore, rebuked the company for its overseas posting policies, snapped at her husband for trying to calm the situation and, finally, stormed out of the room.

In Singapore

Back in Singapore, Paul never gave the Tsus a second thought until three weeks later, his administrative director, Tan Hock Lye, came to him with a plan that would bring back several of the company's regional executives to Singapore. The company is also planning to introduce a comprehensive system of video conferencing between the regions and headquarters.

Hock Lye had listed the overheads for keeping eight or nine senior managers permanently overseas and pointed out that several other companies had taken advantage of the centralization made possible by advances in modern communications technology.

Both privately to Hock Lye and later, at an executive committee meeting, Paul voiced his objection to any such arrangements. And there the matter rested for the moment.

Paul toured the other Asean countries to identify suitable factory locations. When he got back, he learned that news of the centralization initiative had leaked to some of the regional managers and that Daniel and another manager had signaled their interest in returning to Singapore.

Daniel in particular pointed out that he had an able manufacturing manager who was a Brazilian and who was fully capable of dealing with emergencies that might arise in the components factory in Sao Paulo. His own job entailed a general management overview as well as liaison with the Singapore headquarters; a function which he felt he could perform equally well from Singapore. Unfortunately, Paul had viewed the job of a regional manager as much broader than this.

At the next management meeting Paul felt himself the victim of an organized move by Hock Lye and Ronald, the personnel manager.

Hock Lye produced a detailed plan for centralization that would yield considerable benefit in terms of cost savings and streamlining of the organization. Ronald added that he was having problems finding replacements for most of the overseas managers, who would be due to return to Singapore under the job rotation system already in place.

Rotation of managerial staff allowed managers to have two years stints abroad. Most of the overseas stations were located in developing countries where labor was cheap. They had little appeal for many managers who had long-standing impression that the system was a way to send the less favored individuals to Siberia. Daniel had been away from Singapore for five years already, although the initial understanding given to him was that he would only be in Sao Paulo for two years.

Paul responded by saying that they were not in business to find easy ways out of personal problems but to act in the long-term interests of the company. "Brazil is Daniel's responsibility. He is far too valuable to work in Singapore, thousands of kilometres from where the action is," he said. "It is only his wife who is dissatisfied with life in Brazil, and her husband is willing to let her return to Singapore". Paul, being a 53-year old bachelor, could not understand why this woman was especially possessive.

One month later, Ronald came to Paul in his office and said that Daniel had been offered a job in Singapore by one of Sinlect's competitors. Paul frowned and asked for further details. "Well, if we have to lose him I suppose we have to," he said.

"You did say, at the last management meeting, how valuable he is to the company," Ronald tried to remind him.

"Yes, yes," Paul replied, "But no company can keep everyone it would like to keep."

"There is something else, however," Ronald continued, "S. Singam (the company's man in New Delhi) wants to return to Singapore after only a year in India. He has found the recent trouble there too threatening for his family. He has been identified as one of our high fliers and we could easily lose him too."

"It's your problem, Ronald," Paul said. "You are the personnel manager."

"Well, I am trying to do my job in trying to persuade you to take a more flexible attitude toward videoconferencing and bring people back from the field." Ronald explained. "Here is a report I have prepared, after consultation with Hock Lye, on how a more centralized structure would affect our personnel policies."

Paul took the report away and read it. He was still unconvinced. It seemed to him to go against all his convictions that there was no substitute for on-the-spot management worldwide. On the other hand, if he remained entrenched in his position, he was going to lose experienced managers the company could ill-afford to lose.

At the executive meeting, Paul reiterated his stand that in no way should video communication substitute on-the-spot management. He believed that no one, including himself, was indispensable and that in the case of Daniel Tsu, it was better to lose his well-thought-of managers than to lose the control of Sinlect's worldwide network. Hock Lye knew that once the CEO had made up his mind, it was useless to refute his decision. As expected, Daniel tendered his resignation the following week and Paul immediately asked Ronald to fill the vacancy.

19

That's Entertainment!

Japan

Much has been written about Japan and its people: myths and misconceptions, truths and facts. The cliche "economic miracle" is one apt way to describe Japan. And although there are no business schools in Japanese universities, much — perhaps too much — has been written and is still being written on Japanese management practices and philosophy.

Like every race and nationality, the Japanese are labeled by stereotypes which outsiders find convenient for identifying them. To varying degrees of truth, the Japanese have been stereotyped as polite, proper and bowing workaholics, lustful men in search of *geisha*, demure and submissive women, over-pressured children who commit suicides, *ninja*, *samurai*, *kamikaze* pilots and quality-conscious innovators.

The Japanese have been described as "groupy" people, who have strong identification with their work team, department and most of all, their company. A significant number of Japanese still mention their company before mentioning their profession, when they introduce themselves. It is customary for Japanese employees to visit their bosses on New Year's Day. Not to do so would be considered rude and disrespectful. After-work recreation is also shared with colleagues and superiors. In other words, the company is a major social group in the lives of many Japanese.

The act of visiting one's superiors on New Year's Day is also a manifestation of another key value in Japanese culture: that of respect for elders. The authority of one's elders — whether boss or parents — is usually readily accepted, and obedience to elders follows as a natural consequence.

The superior subordinate relationship at work is a parallel to the parent-child relationship at home. Even in the organization structure, the parent-child parallel is discernible. The Toyota Motor Corporation is one such example. Twelve companies, called members of the Toyota group, are attached to the Toyota Corporation. All members work together closely to export and sell Toyota's products, and to supply spare parts and materials to the Toyota Corporation. Executives of one member company may be transferred to another company within the group when the need arises.

Traditionally, the Japanese have expected women to be subordinate to men. At home, the husband is the head of the family. At work, many female employees — even though they may be university graduates in executive positions — still clean the desks of their male colleagues every morning. However, the social status of Japanese women is doubtlessly rising. Nearly "95% of Japanese women are high school graduates, and 36% have junior college or four-year college degrees," said a senior official in the economic planning ministry in an interview with *FORTUNE* magazine. The number of women who wish to be a *geisha* is correspondingly dwindling. But the bar, a Japanese institution, is well and alive.

It is the practice of many Japanese men to adjourn to the bar after a long day at the office. The bar is a place for relieving all the tension which has built up during the day. Barmaids keep the men company, listening to all their woes and frustration. The barmaid's job is to serve drinks, sympathize with her customers and make light conversation when necessary. Obviously, the customer is king, and the barmaid takes a subservient place.

Henry Faulkner

Henry Faulkner works for Royal Chemical Industries, a British manufacturing company which is well known all over the world.

RoyalChem is the maker of a dazzling variety of chemical products which range from car waxes to shampoos, paints, pharmaceuticals and detergents. RoyalChem is a household name in England and many other countries, including Malaysia, Taiwan, Australia and India.

In England, only the best and brightest graduates are employed by Royal Chemical Industries. Employees perform different and diverse functions. The functions include personnel and wage administration; accounting; research and product development; production; buying; marketing; training and general administration.

Three departments — the buying, marketing and research and product development departments — employ graduates who have been trained in chemistry or chemical engineering. Such qualifications are necessary because of the specialized nature of the research and development work. Buyers need to have in-depth knowledge of chemistry to understand the hundreds of raw materials (chemicals) which RoyalChem uses for its products. Marketing officers need background knowledge of chemistry to be able to understand what goes into RoyalChem's products and what makes up their competitors' products. Such understanding helps them market RoyalChem's products more effectively.

When Henry started to work with RoyalChem, he worked in the marketing department. Five years later, he was transferred to the research department because it was thought that he could, as a researcher, apply his market knowledge and use his good relations with the marketing department. Three years after that, Henry was offered the job of heading the Buying department. He became a key figure in RoyalChem in that all the chemicals which RoyalChem used were approved and bought by his department. Before approval, however, the buyers would read the available literature on the chemical and often send samples of it to the laboratory for tests.

As head of the Buying department, Henry was much sought after by chemicals suppliers who wanted to market their products. Henry recognized the importance of having good relations with suppliers; he might get to know of new chemicals earlier, and might have to put up with fewer delays in delivery. RoyalChem's suppliers originated from various countries, among them England itself, Germany and Japan.

Although he had visited many of the suppliers, Henry had never been to Japan. Two representatives of the Japanese suppliers had,

That's Entertainment!

however, visited RoyalChem. The first was Mr T Ogata, senior marketing manager of Izu Chemical Company. Although Mr Ogata seemed reticent at official meetings with Henry and the other managers of RoyalChem, he was always cordial and appreciative of the hospitality shown to him. Henry even took Mr Ogata to a pub to show him what this British institution was like. Mr Ogata enjoyed the pub visit, and promised to take Henry to a Japanese pub when he went to Japan. Henry was careful to maintain good relations with Izu Chemical, because it produced many of the chemicals which were important for RoyalChem's products. Izu Chemical also charged competitive prices for its chemicals, and Henry hoped that its prices would continue to be that way. The second Japanese man to have visited RoyalChem was Mr K Abe, a sales manager from Matsuda Chemical Company. Before leaving Britain, Mr Abe invited Henry to visit Matsuda Chemical.

When Henry discussed the invitations with RoyalChem's director, the latter thought that a visit to Japan would be timely. After all, there were six companies to be visited. At the same time, Henry could also explore the possibility of exporting more of RoyalChem's products to Japan. Henry was very excited about the business trip. Much less enthusiastic was his wife, who, although accustomed to her husband's absences from home, was afraid that his suppliers might also supply him with a *geisha*. Henry laughed about her fears. "There are very few *geishas* left in Japan," he teased her, "And besides, many Japanese women now work in offices". Henry reassured his wife that he would not be unfaithful. "What silly fears," he thought to himself on the plane, "Some of the most proper people on earth are Japanese".

In Japan

Henry's first meeting with Mr Ogata was pleasant. Henry found the Japanese very polite and proper — just as he expected them to be. Henry learnt a great deal about Izu Chemical and identified several other chemicals which RoyalChem did not as yet import, but would be very much interested in trying out.

After dinner, Mr Ogata sportingly reminded Henry of his promise to take him to a pub. Tired from his flight, Henry asked, "What about tomorrow?" "I will arrange a full program for you," Mr Ogata replied, with his usual slight smile. Back in his hotel, Henry found a few books and comics in the drawer. He was shocked when he saw that some of the Japanese comics contained some very explicit and lewd drawings.

He recalled his amazement earlier that day when he had passed a little coffee shop in which there were at least two dozen Japanese men who had their heads buried in comics. "So that's why," he laughed.

The next evening, Mr Ogata and his superior whisked Henry to a posh-looking bar. "This is our pub," Mr Ogata proudly announced. Some hostesses were to keep the men company. Henry felt uneasy because Mr Ogata and his boss talked to the hostesses as if they were their sweethearts, and because the hostess who was assigned to him was getting too familiar for his liking. But he did not quite know how to react. The thought of his wife made him feel guilty, somehow.

After Mr Ogata and his boss had got high on liquor, they told Henry, "The best entertainment is yet to come, Mr Faulkner". Henry grew more apprehensive but felt that he had to be polite, so he said, "Yes, can we go now? I can hardly wait to see what it is". He just wanted to get out of the bar.

So Mr Ogata and his boss took Henry to a "performance". "It is one of the best," they enthused. To his mortification, Henry found himself at a strip-tease show. He felt faint and wondered if he should leave. But that would be considered very rude by his hosts, he thought. Even if he did walk out, how many of such "entertainments" could he walk out of? After all, he had to spend ten days in Japan. "This is pornography, not art," he muttered to himself. After the performance, Mr Ogata's superior, still high on drink, asked Henry if he needed company for the night. That could also be arranged. Henry quickly declined.

Back in his hotel room, Henry was perturbed. He thought these people were repressed, and they were not really as proper as they appeared to be. But on the other hand, Japanese literature and art were often erotic, so maybe it was just a cultural difference. Henry was not sure if he should just bear with all the entertainment — whether he should simply adapt to the culture. But he felt guilty about doing so. Perhaps he could explain to the Japanese suppliers that he did not want that kind of entertainment, and that lunches and dinners would be enough. He was not confident about giving such an explanation. It might offend his hosts and the excellent relations between RoyalChem and the six Japanese companies might sour. However, he had promised his wife he would be faithful, and he felt that the promise included staying away from temptations. Henry knew that he would not be able to sleep until he had thought of a way out of this quandry.

20

Intronic's Problem Tree

In 1980, Yahya Ibrahim graduated from the University of Edinburgh with First Class Honors in Electrical Engineering. After graduation, he returned to his home in Malaysia with the intention of going for graduate studies if the opportunity arose. It did, for a few months later, Yahya was awarded a government-sponsored scholarship to obtain his MSc at the California Institute of Technology (Cal Tech) in the United States.

Since Yahya's studies were financed by the Malaysian Government, he had to serve a bond of five years after graduating from Cal Tech. The Ministry of Trade assigned Yahya to a manufacturing company in Kuala Lumpur (the Malaysian capital). Yahya proved to be an able and serious worker, and he gained the favor of the company's General Manager. An excerpt from the General Manager's report to the Ministry of Trade on Yahya's performance reads as follows:

> Yahya is a brilliant engineer. He has tremendous potential and a positive attitude to work.
>
> In the past year Yahya has, in his position as factory manager, successfully instituted several work improvement programs in our factory. His weakness, however, is that he is impatient and rather short-tempered. This may be the result of the perceived intellectual gap between his subordinates and himself.
>
> I recommend that Yahya be given wide exposure to the manufacturing industry in general. This will allow him to gain

necessary experience expected of a top-notch leader in the next generation of manufacturers in our country.

Right about this time, the Ministry of Trade and Industry received word from one of the manufacturing arms of a government statutory board that the general manager of a small government-supported factory in Port Dickson (about 100 km away from Kuala Lumpur) would be retiring soon and they needed help. Could the Ministry recommend a replacement?

Four months later, at the age of 27, Yahya became the general manager of Intronics.

Intronics is a small factory assembling small electrical motors used in toys and controls. It has 80 factory operators and 15 management staff. The employees do not belong to any union and the racial mix in the factory is roughly 50% Chinese, 40% Malay and 10% Indian.

The organization chart of the company is as follows:

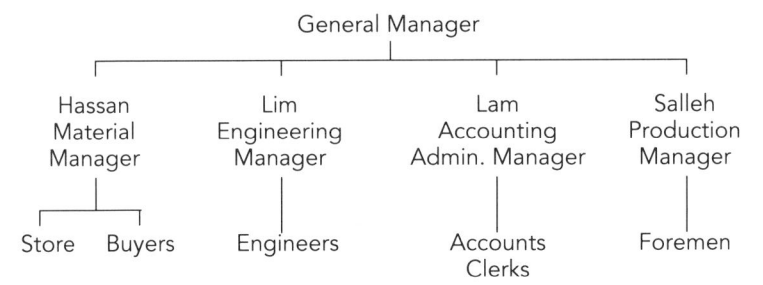

```
                        General Manager
        ┌───────────────┬───────────────┬───────────────┐
     Hassan            Lim             Lam            Salleh
    Material       Engineering      Accounting      Production
    Manager         Manager        Admin. Manager    Manager
    ┌────┐             │               │               │
  Store  Buyers     Engineers       Accounts        Foremen
                                     Clerks
```

Figure 1   The Organization Chart of Intronics

All four managers are in their early forties. Mr Lam, the Accounting and Administration Manager is the longest-serving manager with 12 years in Intronics while Mr Lim, the engineering manager had served at least 7 years. The outgoing general manager had run the factory with a laissez-faire approach. Most of the operators have been with the company for more than 5 years and everyone called the managers by their first name or just the surname. Lim acted for general manager whenever he was away.

Intronics was already in a mess in Yahya's mind when he started work. Discipline was poor. When he turned up at 8.00 am, the production workers were only beginning to trickle in. None of the managers were even in their office.

Intronic's Problem Tree

On the previous day, he had been introduced to the employees by the outgoing GM and had attended a farewell lunch function in the canteen. After that, Yahya was given a briefing of the company's history and organization structure, and a tour of the factory. He had noticed that the factory layout was not efficient and machinery was old. As he left the factory on the previous evening, Yahya also noticed that an old tree just outside the main gate of the factory was obstructing the view of drivers leaving the factory.

Yahya called a meeting with his managers and announced that the factory was 'old-fashioned and that Intronics would be turned into a model factory among those under the government's manufacturing arm. He would also be holding weekly meetings with the managers on Friday mornings.

The changes came fast and thick. Lam was asked to order a time-clock and to issue cards to all employees as soon as the clock arrived. Lim and the Production Manager were asked to work on a plan (proposed by Yahya himself) to re-lay the production lines. The Store Manager was likewise asked to re-lay his stores (again based on Yahya's plan) and to implement a new record-keeping system within a month. Furthermore, Yahya would take a factory tour every morning and implement changes along the way.

While there were stifled protests and complaints, the employees generally obliged and production rose substantially.

The turning point came after six months. At the end of a weekly meeting, Yahya said, " The rotten tree outside the gate is an eyesore and is obstructing the view of drivers. Lim, since you're the engineering manager, can you have it removed?"

Lim exclaimed, "What? Remove the Datuk-kong tree? Are you mad? Don't you know that Datuk-kong lives there and it is he, who is looking after the well-being of the factory? Remove it? That must be the craziest thing that I have heard all week!"

Yahya's face flushed with anger, retorted, "Mr Lim! We are now living in the 1990s! There is no such thing as Datuk-kong or whatever spirit that you are talking about. This is pure superstition".

Lim interrupted, "Superstition? When Hassan's daughter was down with fever and the doctors could not find a cure for her, he prayed to the Datuk-kong and his daughter recovered immediately. Ask him, ask him", Lim said, pointing his finger fervently at Hassan.

Hassan affirmed, "Yes, yes, without the Datuk-kong I do not know what would have happened...." " "As far as I am concerned, the tree will have to go by our next meeting" said Yahya angrily.

It is the belief of many Chinese and Malays that Datuk-kong is the spirit of a kind man who has chosen to remain in this world after his death to help the needy. It normally dwells in an old tree or rock. It makes this known to a needy person in a dream. The news of its existence is spread by word-of-mouth very quickly. When the tree or rock is destroyed or removed, the Datuk-kong will normally punish the person who removes it from its residence. The Datuk-kong is considered to be a local deity by its believers.

Lim refused to remove the tree for several weeks and the grapevine gave its support to him. Finally, Yahya gave him an ultimatum to comply or resign.

Lim had the tree chopped down with outside help (nobody from the factory was willing to do it). Before that, he prayed and made offerings to the Datuk-kong, explaining that he had to do as Yahya ordered because he needed the job to support his family.

Soon after, one of the production workers fell sick for a week. She recovered but there are rumors that she had had a dream when she was sick. In her dream, she had tried to pray to Datuk-kong but it was not around anymore.

Sick leave started to rise. There were also whispers among the operators that they felt a sense of unease, an occasion when going to a particular toilet alone. Had it become haunted?

Everyone attributed all these to the loss of the patronizing Datuk-kong.

Four months later, Lim handed in his resignation. A new electronics factory had started recruitment and together with Lim, Intronics lost another 13 girls in the first month alone. Yahya was certain that this was the beginning of an exodus and unless something was done immediately, Intronics would have a very serious turnover problem in its hands.

21

Goodshoes (Bangladesh) International

Bangladesh: The Land, History and The People

Bangladesh, a low-lying riverine deltaic land located on the northern coast of the Bay of Bengal, is surrounded by India with a small common border with Burma in the Southeast. With an average elevation of less than 600 feet above sea level, the country is criss-crossed by the many branches and tributaries of Ganges and Brahmaputra rivers. Before 1947, the geographical territory now known as Bangladesh was known as East Bengal and was a part of British India. In 1947, India gained independence, but not as one nation: the British Raj partitioned India and created the new nation Pakistan, a homeland for the Muslims of India. East Bengal became a part of Pakistan and became known as East Pakistan. But only after 24 years of combined existence as a nation, East Pakistan gained independence from Pakistan in 1971 through a liberation war that lasted for nine months.

Bangladesh is a densely populated country: an estimated 100.5 million people live in an area of 143,998 square kilometers. About 86.2% of the people are Muslims, Hindus with a population of about 12% constitute the largest minority group. The rate of literacy is only 23.8%, although in urban areas, it is reported to be about 40%. Bangladesh is one of the world's poorest nations with a per capita income of about US$130.00 per year. It is mainly an agrarian country with a small industrial sector. About 85% of the total populace are farmers living in rural areas. A large proportion of them live under the poverty line. The urban dwellers, who account for roughly 14% of the population, consist mainly of industrial and white-collar workers employed by industries, private and public sector enterprises, the service sector and the government.

In the Constitution of post-liberation Bangladesh, secularism, nationalism, democracy and socialism were described as the four cornerstones of state policy. In later years, the Constitution underwent several amendments. In 1986, Islam was declared the state religion and secularism as a state policy was abandoned. However, people belonging to other faiths are allowed to practice their own religious beliefs without fear or hindrance. Bengali is the national language of Bangladeshis, but English is also used quite widely.

Bangladesh Culture

As a people, Bangladeshis boast of a rich cultural heritage. They are fond of fine arts, music and literature. They are generally very docile and mild-natured. Although a majority of the people are devout Muslims, they are not fundamentalists. Bangladeshis prefer to identify themselves as "Bangladeshis first, Muslims later". They take immense pride in their past glories: reminiscing about the glorious past of their ancestors is one of their favorite pastimes.

Bangladeshis are highly politicized: they like to talk about politics of any kind, any time and any where. Although they prefer an easy-going, simple leisurely lifestyle, their emotions can be stirred very easily. Islam and Bengali nationalism are very dear to them and any insult to these two can result in very grave consequences. There are about 165 political parties in the country, and capitalizing on the general nature of average Bangladeshis' mental make-up, these parties, on many occasions were able to create political trouble out of very mundane issues. Traditionally, a materialistic attitude toward life and living had been looked down upon by Bangladeshis who, generally, are a contended people aspiring for a simple life.

However, it has been alleged that after the independence of Bangladesh, her people's traditional values gradually eroded, mainly because of economic hardship.

Goodshoes (Bangladesh) International

Goodshoes (Bangladesh) is one of the oldest multinational corporations

(MNCs) operating in Bangladesh. Originally known as Goodshoes (Pakistan), it assumed its new name when Bangladesh became independent in 1974. Of the 20 MNCs operating in the country, Goodshoes is the only company where the equity of the parent company is 90%. (When it first started its operation in early 60s, the parent company's equity was 100%). In 1979, this company accounted for 68% of the total domestic output of shoes in Bangladesh. Over the years, several domestic shoe manufacturers started manufacturing shoes in the country. However, they failed to bring about any noticeable change in the market share of Goodshoes, which continued to dominate the local shoe market.

Like many other MNCs operating in Bangladesh, Goodshoes faced an uncertain future during the first few post-independence years. The first Industrial (Private) Investment Policy of Bangladesh announced in July 1972, set various limits on private investment. This was mainly due to the constitutional commitment of the then government to create a socialist economy in Bangladesh. Shortly after independence, the government of Bangladesh embarked on a massive nationalization program: it nationalized all industrial units in three large-scale industries namely, cotton textiles, jute manufacturing and sugar manufacturing. The government also took over public ownership of all industrial units with assets over 1.5 million takas (US$50,000) which were abandoned by Pakistanis. As a result of these actions, the private ownership of fixed assets in the industrial sector stood at a meagre 14%. While the nationalization policy of the government did not affect the operation of the MNCs, there was an apprehension that in future, these MNCs could also be nationalized. However, political changes brought about by a series of military coups and counter-coups in 1975 resulted in a discernible change in the economic policies of Bangladesh. The new regime was not very keen on establishing a socialist economy in a country where the tenets of the religion of the masses ran contrary to socialist thoughts. The government actively encouraged the development of private sector industries and the MNCs were assured that they would not be nationalized. There was a marked increase (from 14% in 1972 to 25% in 1977) in the private ownership of industrial assets. The trend continued in the eighties and the MNCs were, to a great extent, relieved of their worries about nationalization.

During the first five years after the liberation of Bangladesh, Goodshoes preferred to maintain a low profile with low-key operations barely enough for the mere survival of the company. Goodshoes was a household name in Bangladesh for its quality, durability, style and fashion. Hence, survival was not difficult. However, the company decided not to recruit new people in place of those who had left the company for one reason or another, develop new styles for their products, or expand their operations. The management deliberately adopted a 'wait-and-see' policy to monitor the events in the political and industrial scene of the country. The changes in 1975 boosted their morale and the company resumed full-scale operations with renewed vigor. By early January 1978, 247 new people (5 managerial, 21 clerical, 193 production and 28 others) were recruited. The company launched 7 new products and expanded their production facilities with a view to increase their capacity by 40%. However, by early 1983, Goodshoes realized that in another two years, further extension of their capacity would be necessary. Two alternatives were considered: (i) expand the existing capacity by another 40%; and (ii) construct a new and more modern factory having double the existing capacity. After long deliberations, the second option was adopted. Certain developments that took place in the Bangladesh economic scene during this time helped Goodshoes in financing their new construction project: in early 1984, Dhaka Stock Exchange (DSE) was reactivated after an absence of about 14 long years. Goodshoes was one of the first MNCs to get enlisted in the DSE. It was decided that 10% of the equity ownership be offered to the local Bangladeshi community. Accordingly, 2,500,000 ordinary shares of Tk 50.00 (US$1.50) each was offered to the general public. The shares were oversubscribed (1 : 43) reconfirming people's confidence in Goodshoes.

The construction of the new factory building was completed in October, 1985. When the operation started in the new factory, Goodshoes had 2117 people in its pay roll. The company developed a new organization chart shown in Figure 1. By early 1989, Goodshoes shares with a par value of Taka 50.00 was traded for Taka 515.00 in Dhaka Stock Exchange.

In developing their footwear products, Goodshoes had always tried to take local cultural and consumer tastes into consideration and come up with products which became popular overnight. Goodshoes products catered to the needs of people belonging to all levels of economic groups. For planning purposes, Goodshoes segmented their market in the following manner:

1. High income families
2. Upper-medium income families

3. Lower-medium income families
4. Low income families
5. Students

Goodshoes essentially adopted differentiated marketing. While a limited number of their products were meant exclusively for the people belonging to the first and the second category of customers representing the upper echelon of the society, the majority of the products were for the people in the lower-middle and the low-income groups. Footwear for the students were limited to only three varieties. Goodshoes developed products using cheap but durable raw materials and sold them at prices affordable by the poor masses. They made sure that none of the raw materials used offended the users. For example, they refrained from using any *haram*[1] ingredient. Each style marketed by the company used catchy but non-offensive Bengali names and traditional motifs.

This extra care about the use of raw materials, design names and design motifs was necessary and very important in the context of Bangladesh. Being Muslims, the majority of the Bangladeshis are very sensitive to any direct or indirect criticism of Islam. When Salman Rushdie's 'Satanic Verses' was published, Bangladeshis at home and abroad were quick to react. Any offending act or derogatory comment against Islam or their national heritage may very quickly enrage the generally friendly, docile, tolerant and easy going Bangladeshis and prompt them to resort to disorderly behavior. It must, however, be noted that under normal circumstances, an average Bangladeshi is neither a fundamentalist nor a chauvinist: but he does become one under insinuating situations. And with so many feuding political parties in the country, creation of such a situation does not require any special quality: one rumor is more than enough. Several past incidents bear testimony to the fact that Bangladeshis get carried away very easily.

Being in Bangladesh for such a long time, Goodshoes management had been well aware of these characteristics. Hence, it is not surprising that Goodshoes executives spend a lot of time and effort in new product development. This caution had paid them off over the years and they are keen on remaining cautious about these sentimental issues.

---

[1] *Haram* means forbidden. Islamic tenets forbid Muslims to eat, drink or use any product which is *haram* (e.g., pork, alcoholic drinks) or product which uses *haram* ingredient(s).

Culture and Management: A Casebook

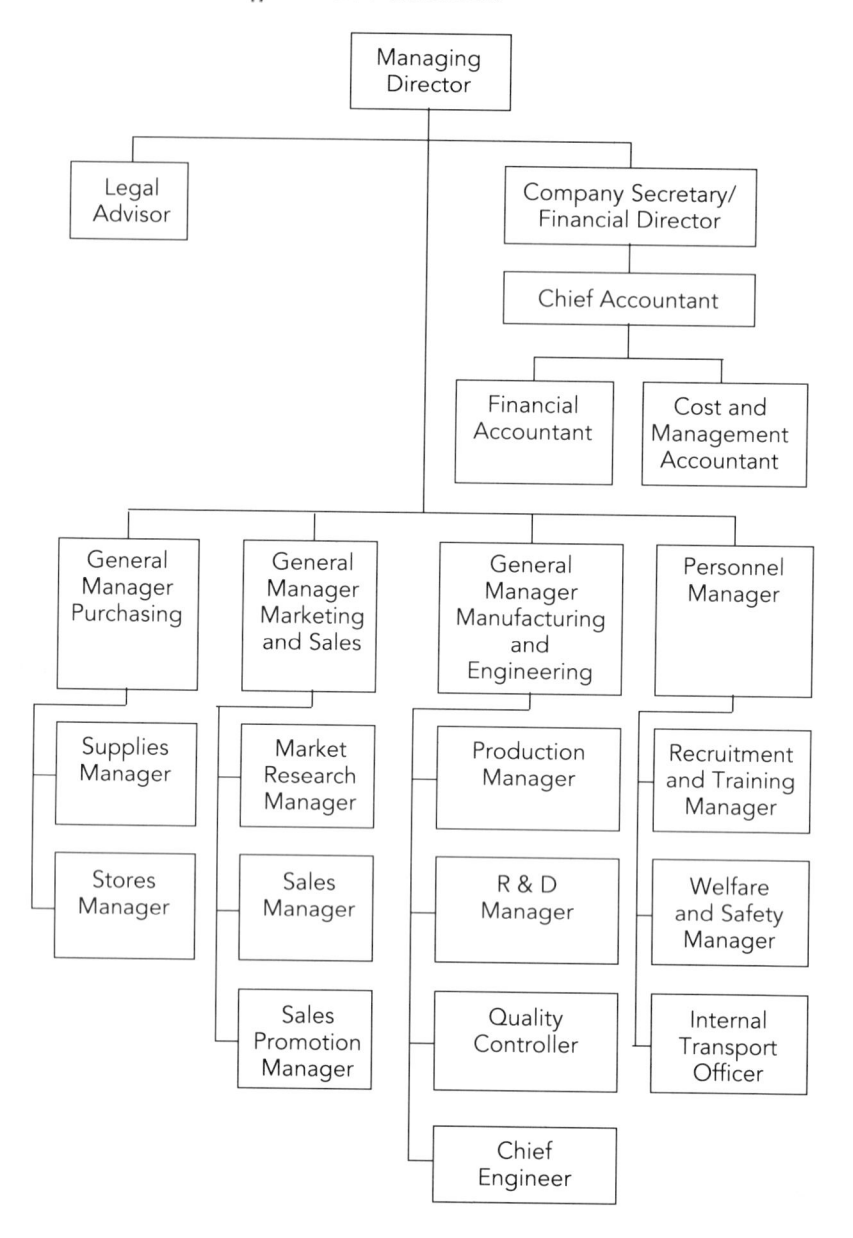

```
                        ┌──────────┐
                        │ Managing │
                        │ Director │
                        └──────────┘
```

Figure 1. Organization Chart of Goodshoes (Bangladesh) International

Reporting to Managing Director:
- Legal Advisor
- Company Secretary/Financial Director
- General Manager Purchasing
- General Manager Marketing and Sales
- General Manager Manufacturing and Engineering
- Personnel Manager

Under Company Secretary/Financial Director:
- Chief Accountant
  - Financial Accountant
  - Cost and Management Accountant

Under General Manager Purchasing:
- Supplies Manager
- Stores Manager

Under General Manager Marketing and Sales:
- Market Research Manager
- Sales Manager
- Sales Promotion Manager

Under General Manager Manufacturing and Engineering:
- Production Manager
- R & D Manager
- Quality Controller
- Chief Engineer

Under Personnel Manager:
- Recruitment and Training Manager
- Welfare and Safety Manager
- Internal Transport Officer

Goodshoes (Bangladesh) International

The Flood Slipper

In 1988, almost the entire Bangladesh was devastated by a massive flood. Being a riverine country situated in the Gangaic delta, from time inmemorial, flood, cyclone and typhoon had been regular phenomenon in Bangladesh. However, only the rural areas and some small towns were affected by the recurring floods which generally lasted for a short time during the monsoon seasons. But the 1988 flood was the worst in recorded history. It inundated almost the whole country, including the capital city Dhaka and lasted for quite some time. Experts predicted similar devastations in the near future as well. Goodshoes decided to develop a new slipper that would be suitable for use in flood waters. The design department came up with a new product and named it *Bannya* meaning flood. This new slipper resembled one of their existing products excepting that it used a new raw material which would facilitate its use in flood waters. However, to enable the customers, many of whom were illiterate, to identify the product easily, the graphic arts department was asked to develop a new motif that would distinguish it from the existing products. Accordingly, a new motif that resembled a Japanese chandelier with the word Bannya appearing below was developed. Goodshoes management was happy with the design, the name and the identifying motif of the product which is shown in Figure 2. They were confident that these would be linked by the people and the product would gain popularity in no time.

The product was launched in early June, the beginning of the 1989 monsoon season. As expected, the product became popular overnight. But just after a fortnight of its launching, a local paper reported that the motif used in the slipper bore resemblance to the calligraphy of Arabic word of *ALLAH* (GOD). Within no time, there were violent protests all over the country. A few Islam-oriented political parties organized mass protests against the product and the company. They attacked retail outlets selling the product and demanded that the product be withdrawn from the market and legal action be taken against the company. Goodshoes management was branded as enemies of Islam, friends of Zionism and accomplices of Salman Rushdie. Some party leaders even suggested that the company should not be allowed to operate in Bangladesh. Goodshoes management was shocked at the turn of the events. After considering the sensitive nature of the issue, they immediately issued a statement apologizing to the people of Bangladesh and promised to withdraw the product from the market. But this did not

Figure 2 Design of the Motif

pacify the angry mass and the government had to interfere. The entire stock of the product was confiscated. Labelling Goodshoes decision of launching the product as 'unfortunate', 'insensitive', 'sad' and 'unkind to the Muslims', a government spokesman promised that legal action would be taken against the company.

The gravity of the problem prompted the Goodshoes' head office in Belgium to send one of their senior vice-presidents to Dhaka, the Bangladesh capital. Bangladesh, with a population of 100 million is a large market for footwear and the company did not want to lose the market. He sat with the top management of their Bangladesh subsidiary and studied many possible calligraphic versions of the Arabic word *ALLAH* (Figure 3). There was indeed some resemblance to the motif with the calligraphy, although he thought it to be a remote one. After long deliberations with the Bangladeshi executives of Goodshoes he was convinced that it was an unintentional mistake : it was designed by a Bangladeshi Muslim designer who had been with Goodshoes (Bangladesh) for over eight years. The visiting head office emissary was completely baffled. He wondered why it happened and how the situation could be rectified.

الل ا   الل ا

الل ا   الل ا

Figure 3. Possible Calligraphy of the Word ALLAH

This case was prepared by Mr Razzaque, Senior Lecturer at the National University of Singapore.

22

Hotel Le Galant

Mauritius

Mauritius, a tiny island-country, lies in the Indian Ocean, closer to Madagascar than to the East Coast of Africa. By air, it is about four hours from Johannesburg, South Africa or six and a-half hours flight from Singapore. Mauritius has a population of only 1.2 million, made up mainly of Indians; the rest of the population are African, Chinese, European and French.

The landscape includes the coastal areas, with their stunning beaches and quaint fishing villages and lowlands covered with sugar cane. It is said that the dodo bird once rested in Mauritius. Today, one can see only a replica of the bird in the museum in Mauritius. Mauritians are a fun-loving and relaxed people. Their unofficial motto "No problem" aptly describes them.

To the tourists, Mauritius is the dreamland par excellence. All year round hundreds of thousands of visitors flock to the island. Although tourism is its main source of income, Mauritius has a beehive of industries with thousands of skilled Mauritians busily engaged in a spectacular industrial revolution. Investors come from Hong Kong, Taiwan, England, France, Germany, Holland, Singapore, India, Pakistan and from all over the world.

The industrial revolution in Mauritius was started in 1970 with the setting up of the Export Processing Zone. Within two decades, Mauritius

Hotel le Galant

has become a major supplier in the international market of several consumer goods. No sheep has ever grazed on Mauritian grass, yet it is the third largest exporter of woollen knit-wear in the world. Mauritius is definitely on its way to joining the rank of the newly industrialized countries.

Mauritius is considered the Hong Kong of the Indian Ocean or the Fifth "Little Dragon" besides Hong Kong, Korea, Taiwan and Singapore. Despite industrialization and its booming tourist industry, Mauritius has been able to maintain its traditions and cultural values and is very much aware that the key to success lies in not only improving the quality of life for its citizens but also in preserving its multi-cultural traditions and the taste of paradise that its visitors dream of. This case illustrates some of those traditions and how they affect the workplace.

Le Galant

Hotel Le Galant, located in the South-eastern part of Mauritius, is a member of Beach Hopper Hotel Group. It has well-over 100 rooms, most of which are chalet style. Since it is on the beach, and closer to the airport, many tourists prefer to stay at Le Galant. Although it is most popular among the French tourists, tourists of other nationalities also flock to Le Galant.

The facilities and rooms at Le Galant are comparable to those offered by many international chains of hotels. However, at times the tourists coming from western countries have difficulty adjusting to the pace of service offered at Le Galant. To tourists accustomed to prompt, attentive service, the Mauritian staff seem rather leisurely in their movements. Occasionally, some tourists who have enjoyed quick service at other Beach Hopper hotels lose their composure and shout at the waiters. However, they are generally more tolerant to the waitresses.

Hotels in Mauritius prefer waitresses to waiters for several reasons. The customers normally tend to be more patient and polite in their encounters with the waitresses and try to hold their tempers even under extremely trying conditions. The tourists are inclined to give the waitresses some benefit of the doubt when service is delayed. When harsh words are sometimes hurled at them, the waitresses take them with apologies and smiles. The attitude of the waiters is often different.

Generally, the waitresses show concern for cleanliness and neatness more than the waiters do. From the employment point of view, the waitresses are not as demanding as the waiters when it comes to 'terms and conditions' of employment. The cost of maintaining a waitress (in terms of uniform, food, etc.) is relatively lower than that of maintaining a waiter. It is also much easier to employ waitresses than waiters. More grievances are expressed by waiters than waitresses. On the whole the waitresses are more pleasant towards customers than are the waiters.

Traditionally, Le Galant had more waiters than waitresses. The ratio was 1 to 10. Several attempts and efforts were made to attract waitresses to work for Le Galant. The Personnel Manager at Le Galant Mr Garreau went round some of the towns in Mauritius, such as Coor Pipe (pronounced 'Coor Pip'), Port Luis, Rose Hill, Grand Gaube and Mahebourg to seek out candidates for waitress jobs. He even offered Rs 1800 per month (equivalent to US$120 to 130) while the waiters were paid only Rs 1200 per month. Mr Garreau was a new comer to Mauritius. After serving four years in one of the resort hotels in the Mediterranean region, he was sent to Mauritius, with the mission of improving the efficiency of customer service at Le Galant.

When Mr Garreau first reported for work, the ratio between waiters and waitresses caught his attention more than anything else. That was the reason that he gave great importance to recruiting more waitresses. He thought that once he could get a better ratio — perhaps even more females than males — he could deal with other problems more easily. He was convinced that he found the root of the problems. He was confident that he could solve it within the next few weeks.

Mr Garreau was no different from many other Westerners posted to assignments in the Asian countries where strong traditions prevail despite the adoption of scientific methods, modern ways and the overall concern for efficiency. Caught up in problem-solving, Mr Garreau overlooked the cultural barriers erected by strong traditions and beliefs. He did not realize that productivity, efficiency and problem-solving were not the only things let alone the foremost things in the Mauritians' minds.

23

"He Will Come Back"

Diversity

Although it appears to be one country, Nigeria has several sub-cultures. It is said that in Nigeria there are more than one hundred ethnic groups. Thus cultural values differ from one part of the country to another. The cultural aspect of Nigeria is enriched by one major sub-culture, the Yorubas. This sub-cultural group is found predominantly in the western part of the country. The Yorubans are characterized by a high degree of civilization and elitism. It is said that this part of the country was the first to be exposed to outside world through colonization and Christianity. Yoruba language is considered to be the richest language in the world. A particular word in Yoruba may have multiple usages. For instance, *pele* could be translated as "hello", "sorry", "get out of that place", and other meanings depending on the circumstances in which the word is used.

The Yorubans have some typical cultural values of their own. They have great respect for elders. Their respect is shown in the way they greet elders. When they see an elder, women kneel down (*kumle*) while men prostrate (*dobale*) to express their very sincere greetings. They never talk ill of their elders. Thus they show godly-reverence to their elders. There is a strong belief among the Yorubans that if one ill-treats or beats one's parents, one's children will do the same to one. This fear fosters a greater degree of tolerance among people and forces them to respect their elders. If one should curse or have bad feelings toward someone who is on the death-bed, the curse will follow the children of those who have such bad feelings. But if prayers are offered for a person in the death-bed, blessings will follow. In Yoruba, this belief is expressed as *"sepe fum omo tabigbadura fum omo mi iqba ti wom fe ky"*. This case is an illustration of how the Yorubans believe and practice the cultural value of respect for elders.

Some of the public enterprises in Nigeria date from its colonial era. The colonial masters introduced the infra-structure, which includes railway and road transportation, postal and tele-communication services, education and utilities. By virtue of age of these services many employees in these enterprises are usually old, many having 20 or 30 years of service. These enterprises look after the welfare of their employees fairly well. They offer them good retirement benefits.

There is a common belief among the people that all the property of these public enterprises belongs to the government and therefore to the people. So pilfering from government offices is rampant. The things taken away from the offices include typewriters, furniture, electrical items, stationery and so on. Nothing much is done to correct the situation since everyone is involved in this practice in some way or other.

Daniel disappears

Daniel Orafe worked for the engineering division of Nigerian Railways. After eight years of service, he was promoted to senior accounts clerk in the engineering division. The engineering division was headed by an expatriate manager, Ken Ross, who was employed to modernize the engineering division. He was slowly making adjustments to the local culture.

On one occasion Daniel was sent to the bank to withdraw money for the distribution of salaries to employees. The amount was huge. There were no escorts. Daniel went to the bank, withdrew money and instead of returning to the office, simply disappeared. Daniel's supervisor in the accounts department, Sam Etta, waited and waited for his return. He telephoned the bank after two hours of waiting. He was told by the bank's cashier that Daniel withdrew the money about two hours ago. Sam was worried. Since there was no escort, someone might have abducted Daniel. It never occurred to him that Daniel would run away with such a huge amount.

After having discussions with his staff, Sam came to the conclusion

"He Will Come Back"

that Daniel must have absconded with the money. The staff who knew Daniel confirmed the supervisor's feeling. Some staff members were sent out to look for Daniel. They were told by Daniel's parents, friends and acquaintances that they had not seen him since that morning or the previous evening. Sam's worries increased because time was running out: the staff members would be expecting their salaries in an hour or two. The money that Daniel collected was meant for employees of lower-level jobs. These were also the employees who had stayed with the company for decades. Sam finally decided that as Daniel's supervisor, he should finally report the matter to the head of the engineering division, Ken Ross.

Sam met the head and explained the matter to him in a detailed manner. Ken Ross was furious and wanted to act without delay. He ordered Sam to make a report to the local police and sent more staff to look for Daniel.

On his way to his office, Sam met a few employees who had been with the company for more than 20 years. They told him that such a thing had never happened in the company before. They also knew that the money that Daniel had absconded with was due to be paid as salaries to the older employees. Seeing Sam, they reminded him of the cultural value of showing respect for elders and the belief that those who cheat elderly people will not get away easily. Sam told them that Ken Ross wanted him to file a complaint to the police and get Daniel arrested.

One of the older workers told Sam that if an elderly person made a prediction under distress, the prediction would definitely come true. "Remember," he smiled, "that people are more careful in their relations with the elderly. (*ewu fum-fum ni iyi agba*)" Then he made this prediction, "Daniel will come back and return the money." The elderly workers then discouraged Sam from going to the police. In one voice, they said "*ko mi le sum ko mi le wo*" which means, "The boy will not have a minute of rest until he brings back the money". Although Sam belonged to the same culture as the elderly workers did, he could not bring himself to believe that Daniel would return, let alone return with the money.

Sensing that Sam was not convinced, the old men narrated an incident which had happened in another company some months ago. One of the young workers took away the tools belonging to an older employee. Three days later, the employee returned the tools to the owner and apologized, promising that it would not happen again. This happy ending, in fact, was predicted by older employees in that company. Upon hearing about this incident, Sam was fairly certain that Daniel would return.

As Sam walked back to his office, he remembered a similar incident in the company where he worked previously. A young employee, a boy of fifteen, cheated two older staff of some money, but subsequently returned it. However, he was deeply troubled by the thought that he cheated elders — *ori agba mbaja* — and sank into a depression. The family of the boy had to go to the company to beg the old men for pardon. They offered gifts of coconut, oil and salt. The boy became normal only after some religious incantations were recited.

When Sam reached his office he sent a memo to the departments, stating that the salary distribution would be delayed for a day or two due to some unavoidable circumstance. He also apologised for the delay. Then he went to see Ken Ross to inform him of his decision not to report to the police, and the rationale for his decision which was based on his discussion with older employees. He was confident that he could convince Ken without much difficulty. This is part of their discussion:

Sam Etta: Hello, Mr Ross, I have changed my mind and I am not filing the police report against Daniel. I am sure he will come back in a day or two. Even if we file a report, the police would not be able to locate him within a day or two.

Ken Ross: (Astonished by the remarks) Sam, I do not really understand. Time is running short. You should have filed your report by now. I asked you to do it immediately, remember? If we wait any longer, we may not be able to locate Daniel at all. He might leave Nigeria, or worse, he might have already left. I am afraid you are making a big mistake. In our country, if something of this sort happens, we report to the police at once. Why did you change your mind? We cannot afford to sympathize, you know.

Sam Etta: After meeting you this morning, I was on the way to my office when I met some of our older employees. They advised me not to file a report against Daniel even though their salaries had been stolen. Their advice was based on the belief that those who cheat older people will never get away with it and that the cheats are bound to return what they have stolen and seek apology from those who were

	cheated. This is their cultural belief and I respect it. That's the reason that I changed my mind. If you still want me to file a report I will do as instructed, but our older employees may view that as an insult because it runs contrary to their cultural belief.
Ken Ross:	Sam! I really don't know how to react to what you have told me, to this cultural belief. It does not sound logical but it must be based on something, so I cannot just dismiss it. On the other hand, how are we to recover the money? Let me think it over for a while. Anyway, he probably would have got away by now if he wanted to flee Nigeria. Meanwhile if you receive any information on Daniel, please keep me informed. Is there any book on Nigerian cultural values which I might read? If you find one, please pass it on to me.
Sam Etta:	Yes, there is a good book. I have it at home—I will bring it to you tomorrow.

When Sam left Ken's office, both were in deep thought. The question, "What if Daniel doesn't return with money?" kept flashing in their minds. Sam had to prepare some contingency plans before he met Ken Ross next morning. Certainly, he would need some help in making those plans.

24

"After-work relaxation" Culture In Guyana

The Land of the Six Races

Guyana, situated on the North-eastern Coast of South America, is popularly known as, "The Land of Six Races". The six races — East Indians, Africans, Chinese, Portuguese, various people of European descent and the indigenous Amer-Indians — live harmoniously in the country. Each race preserves its cultural values derived from those of its descendants. Although in the making, a truly "Guyanan" culture has not yet evolved.

Guyana's proximity to the United States has led to many Western values being imported and incorporated into the everyday life of the Guyanese. Despite the diversity of the races and cultural values, a set of Guyanese values and practices can be identified. These values reflect some similarities among the diverse cultures. One of the practices is that of "after-work relaxation".

Many Guyanese, male or female, young or old, of Indian, African, Chinese or other descent, participate and enjoy being involved in wide variety of sports and recreational activities. There is an "after-work relaxation" culture. For instance, employees may go to the staff-club to *res up* (a Guyanese expression which means "rest") and "cool out" (relax) after a hard day's work. This often leads to the detriment of "depot" (the pot i.e., the family's food) or "de house money" (the money

"After-work Relaxation" Culture in Guyana

available for the family). This attitude of spending hard-earned money for social activities leads to some social problems, such as, family quarrels, and health problems, such as malnutrition among children.

This "relaxation culture" also magnifies itself in the number of workers who, after work, go to "kick ball" (football), "bounce ball" (basket-ball), engage in some other sports, "keep-fit" in "de park" or jog along "de seawall" (the sea defense wall which protects the capital, Georgetown which is 4 inches below sea level of the Atlantic Ocean).

While some companies provide recreational facilities for their employees others find it difficult to do so, because of the recurrent costs of these facilities. The government agencies and corporations therefore have to invest in facilities which enable Guyanese workers to indulge in their customary after-work activities. Considerable financial resources have to be provided for acquisition of staff club facilities for football, basketball, cricket and athletics.

However, some government agencies contend that "dey d'n 'ave to cause dey deh bad" (they did not have to provide facilities because they did not have the resources). They resisted the pressure from workers for sometime. After they "dey d'n satisfy with" (they did not satisfy with) their negotiations with the government agencies, they appealed to the Minister in charge of government corporations and agencies. The Minister "pick up de red phone, call de chairmen an' tell them dat they betta geh de workers the tings or else he gun see (picked up the red telephone which is used by the Ministers, called the chairmen of corporations and agencies and told them that they should provide the facilities for the workers or else they would be dealt with). Of course, the chairmen had no choice but to divert some of their organizations' meagre financial resources to setting up recreational facilities for workers.

The government saw a number of advantages in providing such facilities although it was an expensive proposition. After all, "you gat fuh geh sometin' fuh get sometin" (you have to give something to get something). The informal relationships that developed between workers in a setting outside the workplace often led to better interpersonal relations among workers, that is, "dey gun get along betta" (They will get along better). Communication barriers were removed and work-related problems were sometimes discussed. This way, corporations can build loyalty among workers. The government authorities also felt that through these activities certain positive attributes such as, the spirit of belongingness and striving for common purpose can be built among the workers.

In essence, this "after-work relaxation" culture besides creating better relationships and team spirit among workers, provided opportunities for people from different levels, races, and different backgrounds to learn and get to know about each other. Thus the government bent on spreading this "after-work relaxation" culture among workers throughout the country. Of course, the government encountered some obstacles. One such encounter is narrated in this case.

Magnum

Magnum Corporation, a British multinational trading company started its trading business in Georgetown in the early 1970s and within a decade of its inception, it expanded its activities, including manufacturing. It employed about 200 workers, mostly production workers. Magnum's activities in Georgetown in the 1980s included: Trading, Warehousing, Franchising, and Manufacturing.

The company was a good paymaster. The wages and salary scales were somewhat higher at Magnum than at many other local and multinational companies. Besides better wage and salary scales, the company also offered a wide range of benefits such as medical and insurance benefits, loans, transportation allowance and subsidized meals. These were standard benefits offered to employees in different countries around the world where Magnum had operations. The corporate policy of the company was to refrain from funding or organizing activities off-the-job and outside the organization. In the past, the company refused to entertain specific requests peculiar to certain countries on the ground that such approvals will lead to confusion and create more problems for the company. Thus Magnum took an universal approach in most of its personnel policies.

Decisions, Decisions

The Personnel Manager, Mr Parris, a Guyanese himself, recognized the interests of Magnum employees in recreational activities and the strong government backing for such activities. He felt that if the company did not take measures to provide recreational facilities soon, they would be

"After-work Relaxation" Culture in Guyana

forced to do so by government directives. So he prepared a proposal containing the rationale, objectives, coverage and the cost of such programs. He went to see the Managing Director, Mr Cummins, to get approval for his proposal. This is how the discussion went:

Parris: Mr Cummins, after much thought, I worked out a proposal for recreation activities for our own employees and brought it for your approval.

Cummins: (After glancing through the proposal), Mr Parris, both you and I know that this proposal does not adhere to our corporate policy on benefits and services for our employees in various overseas operations. I am afraid our headquarters may not approve this project. I am very sorry about it.

Parris: I do recognize that the proposal is contrary to our corporate policy, but the pressure from our own employees is mounting on me. Soon we will be getting government directives. Recently, a governmental agency was asked by the Minister in charge to provide recreational facilities for after-work relaxation of employees. I thought that it would be better for us to introduce the program before we receive such directives. Further, such program is in line with local traditions and culture. The "after-work relaxation" is an essential part of our Guyanese culture.

Cummins: I do not think that we should give in to such pressure. We should stand by our corporate policy. We cannot invest in a program outside our company and off-the-job hours. I remember that the senior executives in one of our Asian subsidiaries, demanded that the company provide them with cars since it was a common practice in that country for multinational companies to offer company cars to their executives. But our corporate headquarters rejected the proposal since it was not in line with our policy. Although they knew the consequences of turning down such requests, they stuck with the policy. Knowing their attitude, I do not think I can get our proposal approved.

Parris: (Disappointingly) If that's the position of our headquarters I don't think we can do much. It is better that I drop this proposal. I will try my best to pacify our employees. I will keep you informed of the government directives if and when I receive them. Thanks for your time.

After Mr Parris left his office, Mr Cummins was still thinking of the subject. He knew that it was not the end of it. He must work out a contingency plan in case the government pressured the company to provide recreational facilities for employees to use after their work hours. He would face an up-hill task of persuading headquarters to agree on his proposal. He could present a strong argument and give them an ultimatum. But he was not sure how to frame a strong argument. Should he emphasize the Guyanese cultural values and the importance of accommodating such values? Should he point out what other companies in Guyana were doing in anticipation of government pressure? Should he take more of an humanitarian approach? Could he use any other approach?

In case his proposal was rejected, what other options he should explore? Such option should satisfy his employees and should not be contrary to corporate policy. Anyhow, he must find funds for this project. Mr Cummins invited Mr Parris to join him in drafting a proposal to be submitted to the headquarters. Parris was happy to note that his boss had changed his mind and that there was a possibility that the project may come through.

Now everything depends on building a strong proposal. What factors should go into this proposal and how to convince the headquarters of the importance of this project is the challenge faced by Mr Cummins. Mr Parris should offer some supporting arguments or suggestions to Mr Cummins. But he was not sure about what he should suggest.

25

Suryodaya Private Limited

Suryodaya Private Limited

Kailash Chandra, the managing director of Suryodaya Private Limited and the members of his top management group were considering the steps they should take to increase the satisfaction of customers who bought Suryodaya's gas stoves. Ramachandran, the sales organizer who was in charge of this product had reported to them a number of consumer complaints, both about the product and the service.

Suryodaya Private Limited was a distributing company dealing mostly with industrial products. It worked as an exclusive distributing agent for a number of manufacturers of industrial products in the Udyannagar area. The company was appointed by a foreign oil company as an exclusive distributor for bottled gas and stoves in Udyannagar city (Gujarat State, India) a large industrial town in Western India. This was the first time that bottled gas and stoves were to be put on the market in Udyannagar. Kailash Chandra expected a very good response toward bottled gas in the city and appointed Ramachandran as the sales organizer for the promotion of this product. He sent Ramachandran to the foreign company's factory for four weeks' training.

The bottled gas which Suryodaya was to distribute, was used through a specially designed gas stove supplied by the oil company. A rubber tube connected the stove with the cylinder. The burner in the stove had several small holes through which gas could be lighted with a match after the cylinder valve had been opened and a switch on the stove turned on.

The amount of gas released could be regulated through the switch, which in turn made it possible to adjust the heat according to the requirement. To turn off the stove, only the burner had to be switched off and valve of the cylinder closed. Lighting or putting out the flame of the gas stove was thus very convenient. It took only a few seconds.

On his return from training, Ramachandran set out to study the market and assess the demand for his product. He tried to examine the cooking habits of the local population. He found that generally Gujarati families took morning breakfast, two meals, and afternoon tea. To prepare meals, they normally used a *sagadi* with coal as fuel. A *sagadi*, also known as *angithi* in some parts of India, is an indigenously made, portable pit. To light the coal in the *sagadi*, a rag dipped in kerosene was put in the midst of the coal and lighted. The *sagadi* was then manually fanned by the housewife for about five to ten minutes till the coal started burning. After fanning, the *sagadi* was placed in an open place where it gave out a lot of fumes and smoke before it was ready for use. The whole lighting operation for a *sagadi* took anywhere between 30 to 45 minutes. Once the *sagadi* was ready, food for the family for one meal could be prepared on it. If necessary, some coal was added in between, but whenever this was done, the housewife had to wait for some time before this added coal caught heat and stopped giving out smoke. If the coal was not completely burnt out by the time that the housewife finished cooking, it was extinguished with water for re-use. The *sagadi* is shown in Figure 1.

For preparing breakfast and tea, usually a kerosene stove was used because it was both convenient and quick as compared to a *sagadi*. The lighting of a kerosene stove took only a minute or so. The burner was heated with the help of *kakdi,* a device made out of wired rags, which was dipped into spirit or kerosene and lighted. After about a minute, air was pumped into the tank, forcing kerosene out of the stove's tank through a small nozzle point in the burner. The kerosene changed into a gaseous form and burned with a blue flame.

Ramachandran also tried to estimate the monthly fuel expenditure of an average Gujarati family. It appeared to him that a family of four or five members, using the *sagadi* and the kerosene stove, spent about Rs.

---

* One US dollars equals to Rs 16.

Suryodaya Private Limited

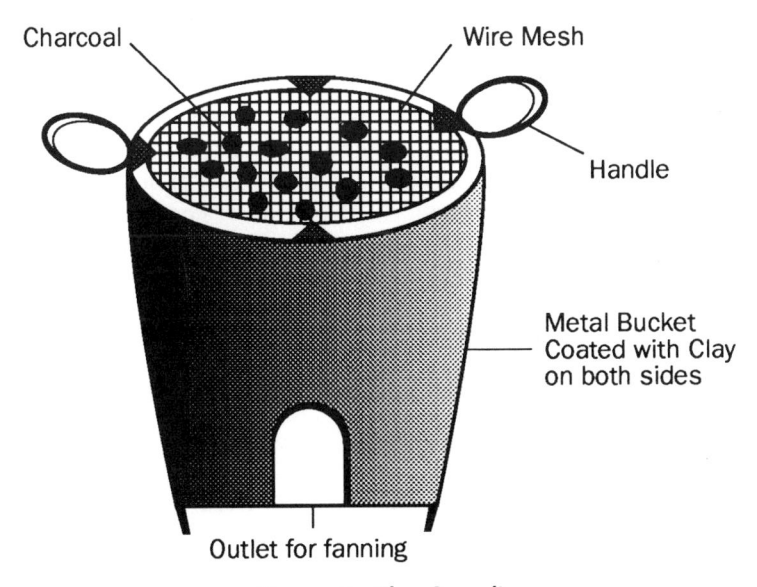

Figure 1 The *Sagadi*

(Labels: Charcoal; Wire Mesh; Handle; Metal Bucket Coated with Clay on both sides; Outlet for fanning)

35 to 40 per month on fuel. If the same family were to change to using bottled gas, it might use about one cylinder per month. As the cylinder was priced at Rs. 57, the expenditure of an average family on fuel was likely to increase by about Rs. 20 per month. Changing to bottled gas also required a substantial initial investment. The user had to purchase a gas stove priced at Rs. 300 and had to maintain a deposit of Rs. 75 with the distributor for the cylinder in use, which remained the property of the oil company. In all, therefore, an investment of Rs. 375 was required for an operable gas stove. This was much higher than the cost of the kerosene stove and *sagadi*. The former cost about Rs. 45 to Rs. 60 and the latter about Rs. 8 to 10. Because of the high initial investment and increased operating cost, it appeared to Ramachandran that the gas service in Udyannagar would have a limited market confined to families who had an income of more than Rs. 1500 per month.

Ramachandran did not have access to any reliable records from which he could obtain the names and addresses of these families in Udyannagar which had an income of more than Rs. 1500 per month. He however chanced upon an article published in a local newspaper which estimated the number of these families to be around 40,000. In the absence of any other source, Ramachandran decided to make use of the telephone directory and the car owners list which was available at the road and transport authority. He assumed that a family which owns a telephone or a car was a potential customer for this bottled gas.

Ramachandran made up a list of 5,000 families from these sources and sent to each a circular sales letter. Simultaneously, he arranged for a number of insertions in the local newspapers. The sales letter and advertisement emphasized the convenience and the cleanliness in the use of bottled gas. Two paragraphs from the sales letter are reproduced below:

> The more convenient, clean, and attractive the kitchen, the greater satisfaction does it give to the housewife. But when the cooking is done with charcoal, firewood, or other old fashioned fuel, the kitchen soon becomes sooty and dirty.
>
> A particularly clean and efficient fuel for cooking and heating is bottled gas, the gas which does not have to be piped and which can, therefore, be used anywhere. No longer need the housewife suffer discomfort in a smoky kitchen. It makes life brighter and will do all her cooking quickly and efficiently.

As a consequence of these efforts, Suryodaya started receiving enquiries. Every day, the Suryodaya office was visited by a number of persons who came to enquire about this new cooking device, to see the stoves, and to have their operation demonstrated.

Ramachandran also started calling on a few families every day. He explained to them the superiority of gas as a fuel, its quickness, convenience, and neatness. From his experience through these contacts, he came to realize that explanation without demonstration was ineffective. His next step, therefore, was to arrange for actual demonstrations. Since house to house demonstration was impossible, he decided to arrange demonstrations in important areas of the city.

In Udyannagar, the co-operative housing activity was very popular. Ramachandran contacted the chairmen and secretaries of these societies requesting them to allow him to give group demonstrations of the gas stove operation in the afternoons when housewives were free. In other areas, he contacted social organizations and arranged demonstrations to larger groups. The demonstrations not only showed the easy operation of the stove, but also included actual cooking by Ramachandran's lady helper. However, the attendance at these demonstrations was usually small; only 10 to 15 housewives went to each demonstration.

Suryodaya Private Limited

In his advertisements, circular letters, and demonstrations, Ramachandran tried to make it clear that gas was as safe as any other fuel. He knew that a housewife or a family head would not like a dangerous appliance in the house. He also knew that the best advertising he could was through word-of-mouth by the housewives who used the gas. He was sure that once a few housewives started using the gas stove others would soon follow.

Ramachandran realized that as this was a new cooking device, it would be some months before it would be accepted by housewives. He therefore planned not to start installing these stoves for a few months. He spent six months promoting the product and booking orders for later deliveries. After six months, he got his first supply of stoves and gas cylinders and started delivery and installation. Within nine months, he had some 2,000 users in the town.

To get the right feel of the problems connected with the introduction and use of this product, Ramachandran and his associates visited homes of users. In addition, those users who experienced any difficulties in regard to the product could register their complaints with Suryodaya's office. Ramachandran maintained a complete record of the problems which he or his associates came across through personal contacts as well as through complaints registered with the office. A review of these records, after few months, showed a number of difficulties which users faced. Some of the major problems which came to Ramachandran's notice are listed below.

Stove Supporters

The Gujarati housewives complained that their cooking utensils did not rest as well on the gas stove as on a *sagadi*. It appeared to Ramachandran that the design of the supporters was not suitable for the utensils used by Gujarati families. The stove supplied to the users by Suryodaya was imported through the parent oil company and had been designed to suit the flat-bottomed pans used for cooking in European countries, whereas the cooking utensils used in Gujarat did not have a flat surface. Since European housewives used pans with handles, they could keep the utensil steady while stirring by holding the handle. This was not possible in Gujarat because the pans used normally did not have any handles. Due to this, the utensils sometimes got over-burned or the food spilt while stirring.

Ramachandran thought that Suryodaya should inform the parent company to make some adjustments to the burner supports to suit local needs. He also thought of bringing this to the notice of the Indian engineering companies who were taking an interest in manufacturing similar stoves. To solve the problem immediately, at least as a temporary measure, Ramachandran asked a local workshop to manufacture a ring to fit the supporters of the stove. The workshop agreed to supply such a ring at a price of Rs. 5 per piece. This, Ramachandran thought, would solve the problem to a certain extent.

Stove Burners

The Gujarati housewives experienced a number of difficulties in preparing certain dishes on the gas stove. For instance, housewives complained that they could not puff wheat *chapati* (similar to mexican bread) on a gas stove as well as they could do on a *sagadi*. Wheat *chapati* is prepared daily as staple food in Gujarati families. Gujarati housewives normally prepare very thin *chapatis*. When they use the *sagadi,* they place a rolled *chapati* on a hot plate and when it is half baked, remove the hot plate and place the *chapati* directly on the live coal in the *sagadi*. Direct contact with the coal puffs up the *chapati*. If the puffing operation was tried on the gas stove, the *chapati* either stuck onto the burner or fell into the spaces between the supporters.

Ramachandran found that this difficulty was due to the burner which had holes on the side, but no hole for a central flame. Accordingly, when a *chapati* was placed on this burner, it stuck at the centre of the burner. It appeared to Ramachandran that this problem could only be solved by designing a new burner which would provide a central flame.

Another complaint of the housewives related to undissolved sugar in the preparation of tea. The Gujarati housewives prepared tea by boiling water, milk, sugar, and tea leaves together and after it had sufficiently boiled poured the tea through a strainer into cups. They complained that while using the gas stove some undissolved sugar settled in the centre of the utensil. Ramachandran felt that the sugar settled in the centre of the utensil because of the curved base of the utensil. Again, because the burner did not have a central flame this portion of the utensil did not receive enough heat to dissolve the sugar settled there. Ramachandran learnt from a local manufacturer that a new burner with provision for a central flame could be manufactured and made available at Rs. 39 per piece.

Suryodaya Private Limited

The Gujarati housewives also complained that certain dishes prepared on this stove did not taste good. Ramachandran believed that this might be due to the uneven spread of heat or to a lack of the intensive heat required in the preparation of these dishes. For instance, to prepare a dish called *kichari* (a rice and lentil mixture) on a *sagadi*, the Gujarati housewife would boil the water, then add some salt to the rice and lentil mixture. After boiling the contents for 20 to 30 minutes, she would take the utensil off the *sagadi*. Then to keep the food hot and to help evaporate the extra water left, she would put a few burning coals on the lid of the utensil. The coals would be left on the lid till they burnt out or were extinguished. In the opinion of the housewife, this process gave a better taste to the preparation.

Ramachandran believed that he could do nothing to solve difficulties of this type. He hoped, however, that once the housewife got used to the gas stove she would come to enjoy all preparations made on it.

Constant Attention

While using the *sagadi* or kerosene stove, the housewife could normally do a number of other household activities simultaneously. She would put the lentils or vegetables on the *sagadi* and get away for some time while it cooked. In the event of overflow from the pan, while she was away, the flame in the *sagadi* would not get extinguished. In the case of any overflow on the gas stove, the stove got immediately extinguished. The overflow also affected the efficiency of the gas stove as burner holes got blocked with the overflowed food. The use of the gas stove thus required some change in the working habits of the housewives. Ramachandran thought that there was nothing he could do about it except he hoped that with the passage of time, housewives will get used to it.

More Match Sticks

A few of the housewives complained that the use of the gas stove involved a frequent use of matches. They had to purchase about three boxes of matches as against one when using a *sagadi*. Though it was a minor matter, Ramachandran was afraid that an average Gujarati housewife might become conscious of this increase in expense as well as the bother of buying matches more frequently. Ramachandran thought that perhaps a stove lighter could be designed to meet this problem.

Apprehensions about Gas

Many people regarded gas as a highly inflammable material. Not only did they fear fire and explosion, but they also believed that the gas was always poisonous. Many housewives argued that if there were children in the house, gas should never be used. They were afraid that the children might play with the valve or switch on the stove, endangering themselves.

Ramachandran explained in his sales letter as well as in his demonstrations that the gas stove was as safe as any cooking device could be. The literature stated that the gas was non-poisonous and non-intoxicating. He added that any leakage of such gas would be noticeable immediately as a special chemical was added to the gas to give bad odor, in case it leaked. If the doors and windows of the kitchen were open, there was very little possibility of accumulation of gas in the kitchen. The literature explained what care the housewife should take in operating the stove. These steps, Ramachandran believed, removed some of the doubts, but still fell short of attaining the acceptance he had hoped for. He believed that stronger efforts were required to remove these doubts. He was sure that once sales gained momentum, the yearly expansion in the number of users would be very large.

There were various other apprehensions about the gas. The elderly women opposed it for different reasons. They associated these appliances with young housewives who, they believed, did not want to use coal as a fuel because of the fear of spoiling hands and clothes.

Among the orthodox sections of the population, the use of the gas was resisted because of religious considerations. This was particularly true of families belonging to the Vaishnava community. Ramachandran was told that a Vaishnava housewife customarily took a bath and put on a clean dress just before entering her kitchen. Nobody was allowed in the kitchen unless he had taken a bath and had clean clothes on. After the housewife had finished cooking, she poured water on her *sagadi* and applied mud all over it. This was done to clean the *sagadi* of all spilt food. In the light of this custom, such a housewife did not like the thought of gas stove because it meant allowing outsiders into her kitchen when the gas cylinders had to be replaced. It appeared to Ramachandran that the resistance could be overcome by perhaps keeping the cylinder outside the kitchen from where the housewife or other family members could take it inside the kitchen. As for spilt food, he thought he could persuade these housewives to use a swab. He also learnt that these

Suryodaya Private Limited

families did not like to have leather or rubber goods inside the kitchen. Unfortunately the stove supplied by Suryodaya was attached to the gas cylinder by a rubber tube. Ramachandran hoped that in time these families would accept this fixture.

No Reserve Capacity

A serious complaint of the housewives was related to the exhaustion of the gas in the cylinder. Many times, the flame died in the middle of cooking because the gas had all been used up. This annoyed the housewives. There was no way in which a housewife could ascertain when the gas would be used up, for the gas cylinder had no indicator on it to show the quantity of gas inside.

Whenever the housewife ran out of gas, she had to notify Suryodaya's distributing depot. Thereupon, a Suryodaya delivery man would go to the user's house and replace the empty cylinder with a new one. As Suryodaya had only one central distributing depot, replacement took about six to eight hours. Sometimes, it even took a day. This created problems for the housewife. The housewife had to keep a substitute cooking device such as a kerosene stove, just in case.

Some housewives suggested that Suryodaya provide a gauge to indicate the quantity of gas in the cylinder. Ramachandran knew that the gas inside the cylinder was in liquid form and a float valve could be installed to indicate the liquid quantity. But such an indication would not solve the problem of the housewife, for she would not know how long the remaining gas would last.

Another suggestion was to provide a transparent portion in the cylinder through which the housewife could see the contents. This arrangement would, however, pose the same problem as in the case of a floating gauge, since the level of liquid gas would not indicate the length of time the gas would last. Moreover, Ramachandran was told by the factory manager that the Inspector of Explosives would not allow such changes in the cylinder.

Ramachandran considered other alternatives to avoid interruption of service to users. One alternative was to have a small cylinder alongside the big one as a reserve. He was informed that as the metal from which these cylinders were made was imported, it would be difficult to provide reserve cylinders. Moreover, a reserve cylinder would create problems of kitchen space.

Another arrangement could be to have a reserve tank within the cylinder itself. Whenever the gas from the cylinder was depleted, the housewife could open a valve controlling the reserve and the gas would come through the main cylinder. This alternative required redesign of the cylinder, which the parent oil company might be reluctant to do. In addition, there would be an accounting problem: when the user switched on the reserve, she could call Suryodaya for replacement of the cylinder, but when the cylinder was replaced, a small quantity of gas would be left in the reserve tank unused and the user would expect to get credit for it. As these cylinders were sent to the factory for refilling, allowance for unused gas would create accounting problems.

To reduce the time between receiving notification from a user and delivery of the replacement cylinder, Suryodaya could increase the staff and vehicles at the central office. However, economy called for a schedule of deliveries rather than individual quick deliveries.

Another alternative was to have depots in different parts of the city. A user could inform the depot closest to him and thus reduce the time lag substantially. But this would involve substantial investment in depots and inventory of cylinders as well as an increase in the distributing costs. Ramachandran was seriously considering appointing sub-agents, who, in return for a small percentage of the commission, would take on the work of quick delivery of cylinders to users located near them.

Suryodaya got a commission of Rs. 10 per cylinder from the parent company, out of which it could pay Rs. 5 to the sub-agent for the cylinders distributed by him in his area. Ramachandran, however, wondered if it would be possible to get sub-agents, at least till the time the gas stove became a popular possession of the housewives. The sub-agents would have to maintain a number of facilities like a showroom (preferably on the main road), a telephone, satisfactory storage and godown facilities to meet the requirements of the Chief Inspector of Explosives, and a vehicle. They would also need a staff consisting of a clerk and a delivery boy. Ramachandran was not sure when the use of gas would reach a figure where it would be possible to have sub-agents who would find it a profitable business. How to overcome the cultural barriers in capturing a major segment of the market was his main concern.

This case was prepared by Dr. Subhash Mehta, Associate Professor at the National University of Singapore.

26

Lebollo In Lesotho

Lesotho

Lesotho is an enclaved kingdom surrounded by the Republic of South Africa. On the map it may look like a tiny hole in South Africa. It is one of the smallest countries in Africa and perhaps one of the poorest in the world. Basotho (the nationals of Lesotho) subsist predominantly on agriculture and depend heavily on the Republic of South Africa for consumer food and employment.

Lesotho has a rich ethnic history. Its founder, King Moshoeshoe was a skilful and sensitive leader who succeeded in building a nation out of several different tribes of Sesotho-speaking people. These ethnic groups in Lesotho include: Bahlakoana, Bakoena, Batlokoa, Bataung, Bafokeng and so on.

The Basotho culture was highly influenced by the early missionaries who settled in the country as far back as 1833. The missionaries provided the infrastructure for education, which explains the country's high rate of literacy (65%). Currently, about 90% of the population is Christian. The constant contact with South Africa was also not without effect.

Of the few customs that are remaining, *Lebollo* which means circumcision, is still widely practiced in the more rural eastern highlands. It gives a young man social status, respect and most important, a license to start a family. Lebollo is a year-long ritual, the most significant part of which is the circumcision ceremony, during which the foreskin of the male organ is cut. This is to be done by the *Ngaka*, a traditional doctor who usually has extensive expertise in this job. The *Ngaka* also acts as the Principal of a 'school' which the young man has to attend after circumcision. The operation is done under no anesthetic to test and confirm a young man's endurance for pain, and symbolically, hardships in later life. The operation is usually done with the aid of traditional herbs to lessen the excessive loss of blood.

Normally, the ritual starts during summer months; this period is considered the orientation period. The young men are prepared both psychologically and physically for the circumcision in winter. The cold weather helps to speed up the recovery of the wounds. Then follows a long period of convalescence until the end of autumn during which lessons on virtues, customs, war techniques, relationships with women and skills needed to head the family are taught. The graduation, which is a very colorful event, is attended by everybody from the surrounding villages, especially women. It takes place in spring. The fathers of the young men usually give a cow each to the *Ngaka* in payment and thanksgiving for the initiation.

Elegant Clothing

Elegant Clothing (Pte) Ltd., one of the South African Group of companies, established a factory in the Leribe district in 1976 as part of the Government's industrialization programme. In 1986, after 10 years of hard work and perseverance, Elegant had become the country's biggest employer and foreign exchange earner. In order to localize its operation, Elegant filled its key positions with locals. Some of these positions included those of accountant, administrative manager, quality control manager and sales manager. The company developed training programmes for mechanics, electricians and other technical staff.

Thabo

Thabo was born in a small village in the farthest north-eastern corner of the country. He was the first son (*Lestibolo*) in a family of six children, a position which conferred great responsibility on him as father's rightful heir and consultant in most family matters.

Thabo attended St. Vincent's Primary School for seven years and moved to St. Joseph's for his secondary education. He did fairly well in the final examination and secured top grades in mathematics. Fr. Jean, Principal of St. Joseph's School showed keen interest in Thabo's progress ever since he entered the school. Fr. Jean advised Thabo to pursue technical education. He was confident that Thabo would be able to make a successful career in engineering.

On Fr. Jean's recommendation, Thabo secured admission in the most prestigious Vocational Training College in Lesotho. The college was located in Leribe district. In the aptitude tests administered by the counselling center in the college, Thabo scored high marks in the sections relating to mechanical engineering. So he was placed in the mechanical engineering programme. After attending college for three years, Thabo graduated with a diploma in mechanical engineering.

Thabo was delighted with the results and went to see Fr. Jean for conveying the results and thank him for his guidance and help. During his conversation with Fr. Jean, Thabo expressed keen interest in receiving some practical training. Fr. Jean referred him to the administration manager of Elegant Clothing who was an ex-student of St. Joseph's. Thabo took the recommendation seriously and went to see the Administration Manager, Mr Matli.

Mr Matli was impressed by Thabo's credentials and accomplishments during the primary, secondary and vocational phases of his education. He gave importance to the fact that Thabo had been recommended to him by Fr. Jean, principal of St Joseph's. Mr Matli was convinced that Thabo would make a good mechanical engineer. Without much hesitation, he offered to make Thabo a trainee in the mechanical engineering department.

After paying a short visit to Fr. Jean, Thabo rushed home to give the happiest news to his father. He thought that his father would be delighted since he would be able to support the big family from his income. On the contrary, Thabo's father went into a shock when he heard of the career plans of his son. When he recovered, he turned to his wife and scolded her for sending his son to primary school despite his objection. If she had not, he would not have to face this consequence. In the village, this would be a source of great embarrassment for him. Following the traditions of his tribe, he wanted his son to participate in the ceremony of *lebollo,* get married and settle down to family life in the village. That would have earned him respect from the villagers. Thabo's father vowed to do everything in his power to "... put sense in the young man's head".

Meanwhile, Thabo accepted the offer and reported for work. He spent a considerable amount of time with Mr Matli, the Administrative

Manager on the first day, discussing job responsibilities and Thabo's future career plans. He was told that he would be rotated on various assignments for the next six months. On completing his probation, Thabo would be placed on a permanent job with full salary and fringe benefits.

During the probationary period Thabo performed extremely well and established good relations with his colleagues and supervisors. Mr Matli was keen to confirm him even before the end of the probationary period. The factory manager agreed with the administration manager's recommendation. Thabo was confirmed as a permanent staff member of Elegant with the title 'Junior Mechanical Engineer'.

Mr Matli saw great potential in Thabo. But something kept bothering him. He came to know of Thabo's position in his family; he guessed that Thabo, being the first son, might have to give up his job in future, to fulfil his obligations to his family. He was afraid that he would lose him sooner or later. Elegant faced problems of getting good mechanical engineers. In order to keep Thabo's morale and motivation high so that he would develop loyalty to Elegant and so that nothing would distract him, Mr Matli gave Thabo some special incentives and personal guidance. A good relationship developed between Thabo and Mr Matli. Thabo looked up to the Manager as his mentor. Since he had a favorable relationship with the Manager and saw potential for himself in the company, Thabo even declined a scholarship offered by the government for a degree in Engineering in the United Kingdom.

The Factory Manager was also impressed by Thabo's intelligence, hard work and loyalty. He nominated him for a special training programme in South Africa, a rare opportunity given to locals. Normally, employees were given such opportunities only after six to eight years of service. In Thabo's case, it took only two years before he got such an offer. Even though Thabo's colleagues were envious of his rapid progress in the company and his favorite-son status, they recognized his expertise and ability to relate to people. Thus, they refrained from raising objections or protesting whenever Thabo was given some special incentives.

During his six-week stay in South Africa, Thabo was exposed to some modern techniques in process engineering. He showed keen interest in learning new techniques and impressed his trainers in the parent company. He knew that on his return, he would have to work independently since he would be the only one who was going to be familiar with the new machine and its operation. Thabo was very much

Lebollo in Lesotho

attracted by the social life in South Africa but he returned to Lesotho without yielding to its temptations.

The factory manager and the administration manager were very happy to see Thabo back in their company. They were confident that they could use his new skills to the fullest. The administration manager had taken a great risk in sending him for training in South Africa and was happy to see his risk being paid off.

The Letter

Eight months after his return from South Africa, Thabo received a letter from his father summoning him to a family meeting urgently. The letter, which had been written for him by a neighbor's son, is shown in Exhibit 1. The English version is shown in Exhibit 2.

Exhibit 1
Letter to Thabo From His Father

Thabo Ngoanaka,

Ke u laela mona ho tla hae kapele ho tla phuthehong ea lelapa ka bokamoso ba hau lapeng lena. Joale ka ha u tseba bophelo ba ka bo tokolang, ke leka ho roalla le sa sele. Ke memme le bo ritata'o moholo ho tla ba teng phuthehong eo, ho imamella ka litsebe tsa bon liqeto tsa phutheho eno. Ke u leleletse.

Ntato
Tseliso Lebenya

Exhibit 2
English Version Of The Letter

Thabo, My son:

I hereby instruct you to come home immediately to attend a family meeting to discuss your future in this family. As you are aware, my health is failing. I am keen to make hay while the sun shines. I have invited all the elders to bear witness to the discussions and decisions that will take place at the meeting. I will expect you.

Your Father
Tseliso Lebenya

Thabo knew from the tone of the letter that it would be important for him to attend the meeting. At the preliminary meeting among the family members, it was decided that if Thabo did not obey his father's wishes about Lebollo, he would have to forego his position as his heir. It was a very difficult situation for Thabo. Although he did not believe in circumcision and the rituals, Thabo was nevertheless unwilling to pay such a high price for his job. However, he greatly feared for his job as he would be absent from work for at least one year; the ritual might require that length of time.

Thabo was in a dilemma. On the one hand, he didn't want to disappoint the factory manager and the administrative manager who put so much confidence and trust in him. They had taken the risk of sending him to South Africa to learn new techniques in process engineering. What would they think of his loyalty if he abandoned his job and went back to his village? Who would replace him for a year or longer? He spent years in education and training to accomplish his goal of making a career in mechanical engineering. What was to become of his own future?

On the other hand, he did not want to disappoint his ageing father. The family looked up to him for leadership and assistance. Who would lead the family in case he decided to stay with Elegant? What would the villagers think of him? Would they call him an ungrateful son? How could he go back to his village for holidays? He might have to sever his relationships with his family and villagers if he disobeyed his father.

Thabo's problem was relatively minor compared to the problem he created for Elegant. If he decided to go back to his village even for a year, he would upset a number of Elegant's activities and plans and delay its move into modern technology in process engineering. Of course it would be a great shock for the factory manager and the administrative manager.

In tears, Thabo discussed his dilemma with the factory manager and Mr Matli, the administrative manager. When they heard Thabo's news, both managers were terrified of the implications for the factory. Thabo's absence for a year would certainly hamper the introduction of new technology. They might have to send someone else to South Africa for six to eight weeks' training to replace Thabo. A whole series of personnel actions would have to be taken within the next few weeks if they decided to grant Thabo a year's leave. In anticipation of Thabo's promotion, they had not renewed the contract of another mechanical engineer. The administrative manager knew how difficult it would be to

Lebollo in Lesotho

attract a good mechanical engineer. They might have to seek help from the parent company in South Africa but there might be problems since very few people would want to leave South Africa to work in the "mountain kingdom".

The administrative manager had anticipated that Thabo would one day leave Elegant but he did not expect that it would come so soon, just eight months after Thabo's return from South Africa, and just two years after completion of probation with Elegant. He was nevertheless very sympathetic with Thabo's case and was willing to do everything possible to help him. He offered Thabo a revised salary package as an inducement to stay. However, Thabo felt that the monetary incentives would never compensate for the loss of his position in society. Later, Thabo met the factory manager who said, "Thabo, we would like you to stay with Elegant. As you know, there'll be many practical problems if we were to "freeze" your job for a year, and wait for your return".

Thabo was asked to meet the factory manager and the administrative manager again after a week. Meanwhile, the two managers planned to discuss the matter at the next management meeting, in two days' time. The factory manager and the administrative manager decided to write a proposal for the management meeting. Such a proposal must be acceptable to both Thabo and Elegant. But they were not sure what they should include in the proposal.

27

The Subordinate Site Engineer

The Housing and Development Board

One of the hallmarks of Singapore's progress since its independence in 1965 is its public housing program. The Housing and Development Board (HDB), the largest statutory board in Singapore, has been responsible for planning and building housing estates for Singaporeans. The HDB has not only built flats; it has also designed and constructed shopping areas, parks, sports facilities and community centres for its residents.

The height of HDB's building activity came in the early 1980s. In March 1987, the percentage of Singapore's population who lived in HDB flats reached 85%. Today, a visit to an HDB estate is a standard item on the itenary of a distinguished foreign diplomat. Tourists can also take in the sites of and savor life in HDB estates in a special tour. The sheer task of building HDB estates is enormous. Although the HDB employs many professional and competent engineers and technicians, much of the work of building is sub-contracted to private construction companies. Workers from these companies are supervised by HDB engineers and technical officers. Among these companies, some have consistently performed well, and have been designated "core" contractors. The "core" contractors in turn sub-contract smaller jobs to other companies when necessary.

The Subordinate Site Engineer

Sun Company

Sun Company is a Housing Development Board (HDB) five-star core contractor under the directorship of C C Lim, K K Chen and A K Yip. C C Lim is the chairman of the board, K K Chen the managing director in charge of the day-to-day operations of the company, and A K Yip is the executive director. The figure below shows the organizational structure of Sun Company.

```
                    Board of Directors
                            |
                    Managing Director
                            |
                    Executive Director
            _____|_____
            |         |           |         |
         Project   Project     Project   Project
         Manager   Manager     Manager   Manager
            |         |           |         |
          Site      Site        Site      Site
         Engineer  Engineer   Engineer  Engineer
            |         |           |         |
         Foreman   Foreman     Foreman   Foreman
```

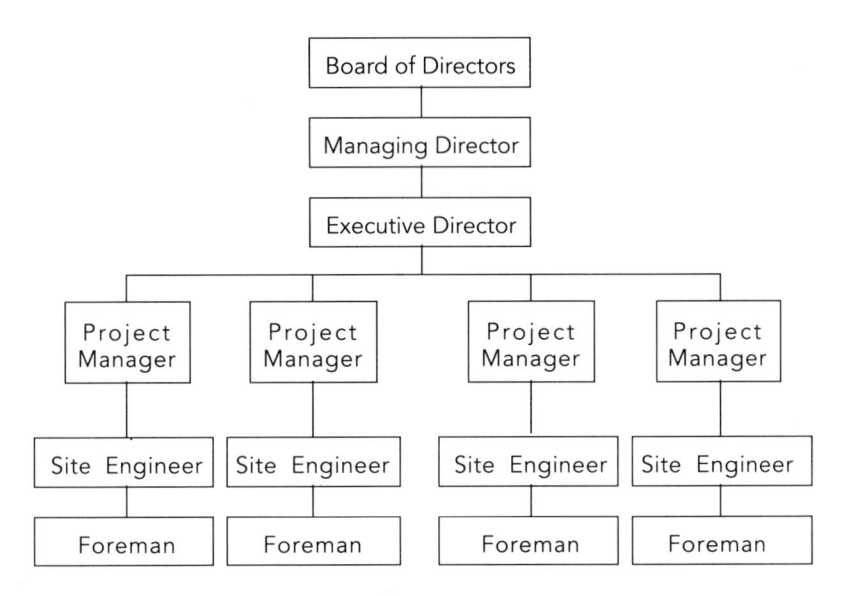

Figure 1. Organization Chart of Sun Company

As can be seen from the organization chart, each project is overseen by a project manager. A project usually consists of a few contract areas under the HDB scheme. To assist the project manager, there is at least one site engineer in each contract. The latter is a requirement under the contract with the HDB. At the bottom of the management hierarchy are the site foremen who report to the site engineers. Prior to the 1983 HDB ruling that every contract worth more than $1.5 million should have at least one site engineer, overall site supervision was the responsibility of the site foreman who received help from a few assistants.

Culture and Management: A Casebook

With the introduction of the new ruling, however, the site engineer was given authority for site supervision. With this authority also came responsibility. The change was not well received by most foremen who, until then, had full authority on each site. Having to report to someone who was likely to be younger and less experienced was an unrelished change. As time was of essence in most projects, there was no allowance for a smooth transfer of power from the foremen to the site engineers.

In April 1988, a fresh graduate from the National University of Singapore, Mr K T Siew was recruited by Sun Company as the site engineer for its project in Jurong East, a new estate on the west part of Singapore. On the first day that he reported for work, Siew was taken to the site by the project manager Mr Kishnani. On reaching the site, Mr Kishnani introduced Siew to the site foreman, Tan and asked him to show Siew all the drawings and contract documents. After the brief introduction, he left the two to acquaint themselves. When Siew asked Tan for a briefing, Tan replied, "I'm very busy right now. I have some inspection to do. You'll find everything you need on the table over there". Without waiting for a reply, he left the office.

For the rest of the day, Siew spent most of his time pouring over the contract drawings and documents and occasionally walking about the site looking over the construction work. Promptly at 5.00 pm, he left the site. From the second day onwards, Siew came in to work at 8.00 am, sat in the office till about 10.00 am, went for a cup of tea, then took a tour of the site. After lunch, it was back to the office again. In the afternoons, Siew alternated his time between the site office and the site, occasionally being called upon to verify certain documents.

The authority for the day-to-day running of the site remained with Tan, the site foreman. Whenever the director Mr Yip visited the site to check on the progress of the construction work, he would confer with Tan only. The relationship between Yip and Tan was fostered since the day Tan joined Sun Company fifteen years ago as an office boy. He subsequently rose through the ranks and became a site foreman under the patronage of Yip ten years ago.

One afternoon in late May, Tan was temporarily unavailable for an inspection of the beam reinforcement before concrete was to be poured. Siew was asked to do the inspection instead. He found that the formwork alignment was out and immediately cancelled the scheduled pouring of concrete that afternoon. Formwork is the mould made to give the shape of a beam or column. As an engineer, Siew knew that each beam and

The Subordinate Site Engineer

column was vital to the structural soundness of a building. He remonstrated the subcontractor for shoddy workmanship and asked the latter to re-do the formwork. The subcontractor was not happy with Siew's decision and a heated argument ensued.

When Tan returned to the site, the subcontractor complained about Siew's 'high-handedness'. Tan then confronted Siew, "Why did you stop them from concreting the beam? Do you know that we will be very far behind schedule because of the cancellation!" Siew replied, "I've checked the beam reinforcement and formwork. It was really a sloppy job. Do you expect me to allow them to continue without rectification? I would never compromise on quality!" Tan, getting red in the face, shouted back, "What do you mean, sloppy! Don't try to be too smart. I'm going to order the concrete right now and pouring will proceed this afternoon whether it rains or shines. Please sign the delivery order when the concrete arrives".

When Mr Kishnani visited the site the following day, Siew immediately mentioned the incident to him. Before he could even finish, Mr Kishnani interrupted, "I know what happened yesterday. Tan has already spoken to the director Mr Yip about the incident and Mr Yip has related the whole thing to me. I know that you are in a very difficult position but the whole thing was a minor misunderstanding. Why don't you try to sort things out between yourselves?"

After the incident the relationship between Siew and Tan became strained and tense. Thinking that it might ease the tension, the project manager asked Tan to relinquish some of his duties to Siew so that there would not be further conflict between them. However, every now and then, there would be squabbles between the two.

Burnt offerings

A common practice on almost every construction site during the first and fifteenth day of the lunar month is for Chinese workers to burn incense, joss paper and make offerings to Chinese deities and spirits. This tradition reinforces the belief that the well-being of the workers on the site would be "spiritually" protected. During the period of the seventh lunar month, the month of the Hungry Ghosts according to local belief, this ritual becomes a daily affair, culminating in a major celebration at the end of the month which includes an auction of religious or auspicious items.

That year, all the subcontractors pooled resources to organize the celebration on the last day of the lunar month. On that particular day, Siew, who had not been previously informed of the scheduled celebration, noticed that the subcontractors had brought in large quantities of joss paper and religious artefacts to the site. At the end of the day, he checked the site store before going home. Siew was responsible for the keys to the store. A duplicate set of these keys was kept in the office for the foreman to use when Siew was away. Inside the store, Siew found several huge stacks of joss paper and numerous bottles of liquor. He suspected that there was going to be a bonfire at the site that night. Siew was angry as no one had informed him of this and the site was full of fire hazards such as timber, tins of diesel and cylinders of gas. Fearing that there might be a potentially disastrous fire, he decided to lock the store. He also removed the duplicate key from the office to prevent any mishaps. After all, he was also the safety officer and all aspects of site safety came under his purview. He did not consult the foreman on this because he was still angry with him.

    The next day, when Siew arrived at the work site, Tan was already waiting for him in the office. As he entered the office, Tan immediately asked him whether he knew anything about the store being locked the night before and the duplicate key being missing. Siew replied that he had locked the store the previous night and taken the key home with him. On hearing that, Tan angrily upbraided Siew, "You knew that all our subcontractors kept their joss papers in our store for the celebration last night and yet you purposely locked it up! What are you trying to do?" Siew replied, "I'm the engineer here and also the safety officer. I will not allow any open fire which will endanger the safety of the site. Anyway, it's against fire safety regulations to have an open fire. We could be charged in court." Tan retorted. "Our men have always been burning joss papers in the seventh month without any problem! Now you come along and offend other people's religious beliefs! I don't know what's going to happen now". "Quiet! I will get you punished for insubordination if you continue to speak in this crude manner!" Siew was by now absolutely furious. But Tan continued, "Our subcontractors and their workers were really mad last night. How do you expect them to cooperate with us in the future? Can you imagine how embarrassed our director Mr Yip was when he came here last night on the invitation of the workers?" Then with a smirk, Tan announced, "In fact, he will be coming here this afternoon, and he wants to see you."

The Subordinate Site Engineer

Siew was shaken. Ever since he joined Sun Company, things seemed to have gone wrong for him. As he prepared to meet the director, he quietly recalled all the events that had led to his predicament.

28

The Governor Goes Crazy

Ethiopia

Ethiopia is one of the least developed nations in the world. Based on Ethiopia's first population census of May 1984, its population is estimated to be around 43 million. About 80% of its population is rural. Its per capita income is about US$120 per annum.

Ethiopia has been plagued by recurrent droughts and famines over the centuries. About 23 famines were recorded during the two and-half centuries ending in 1800, equivalent to one famine every 11 years. The last century was marked by recurrent famines which result in invasion of crop pests, out-break of rinder pests, destruction of cattle, mass starvation and deaths. Many may remember the drought of 1984–85 which caused massive starvation and countless deaths.

Ethiopia is divided into fourteen administrative regions. The traditions and cultural beliefs of its people vary from region to region. For instance, in the Wello region, which is a drought affected area, the staple food consists of a variety of cereals, cattle, meat and milk. They will not eat anything other than these. This belief is based on the teachings of the Bible.

Specifically, the food consumed by the people in the Wello region is known as "Injera", made up of cereal called "Teff". This cereal is found only in Ethiopia. The way "Injera" is prepared is quite similar to the Indian "chapati" or Mexican bread. The flour of "Teff" is mixed with water and then stirred for 10–15 minutes. After that, it is left for two days to be fermented. Once it is fermented, the semi-liquid is spread on "Mitad" (fry-pan) and cooked only on one side.

When the Wello region was affected by drought, many countries rushed massive amounts of rice and wheat, not knowing the food habits of the people in this region. They would rather starve than take rice which did not taste as good as "Teff". The International Aid Agencies had to divert the distribution of rice to more urban areas in the country where the people are accustomed to eating rice.

Such is the adherence to custom by some of the Ethiopian people. The following case illustrates the power of local culture over ideologies propagated by the socialistic government in Ethiopia. The Marxist-oriented military council wanted to replace the traditional values and beliefs with the new socialist ideology and practices.

The Traditional Government Officials

Under the powerful rule of the late Emperor Haile Selassie, the traditions and cultural values prevailed in every aspect of life in Ethiopia. Even the government officials were expected to follow these traditions and values in exercising authority and carrying out their responsibilities. These government officials were self-disciplined (Chewa), followed the religious practices, refrained from doing anything that would be contrary to the norms of Ethiopian society, and were expected to maintain certain amount of dignity in their role as government officials. For instance, they were not supposed to drink in bars or eat in restaurants in their localities. They were expected to observe religious practices and set good examples for the citizens.

When the government officials, such as governors and senior officials, went to work, they were not supposed to walk to work or to go alone. They were always accompanied by attendants which added some prestige to their position. The governors, especially, were accompanied by representatives from various Ministries during their field trips.

Some of the qualities attributed to these governors include ability to decide and lead, show exemplary bravery in times of war (Jegina), and show kindness and generosity (Legasse). Even though they were the highest officials in the Administrative hierarchy, they were expected to show respect for elders. People in a region or locality respected and were ready to lay down their life for those governors and government officials who exhibited the above qualities abundantly and related to people.

The New Government Officials

When the military government took over power from the Emperor, it eliminated the former governors and senior government officials and replaced them with officials and Ministers who backed the military and had leanings toward the Marxist ideology. As a preparatory training, these officials were sent to Soviet Union, East Germany and Cuba for orientation in Socialist system and administration. After receiving three months of training, they returned home to assume their responsibilities as Governors, Ministers, and officials.

Before they were sent to various regions and administrative districts, these officials were invited to listen to a policy speech by the chairman of the Military Administrative Council who is currently the President of the country. The following directives were given to them during the speech:

* Go to the people
* Live with them
* Live the type of life they live
* Tell them that you are their children
* Tell them that you are there to serve them
* Teach them and help them
* Do not forget that you are not sent simply to replace the former feudal officials but to show a radical change.

Shumiye Bekelle

Shumiye Bekelle was appointed as a Governor and sent to the province of Gayint in the region of Oondor, in the Northern part of Ethiopia. Armed with the Socialist ideology, he was excited and wanted to start work without any delay. He was inspired by the speech given by the chairman of the Administrative Military Council. Before leaving for his assignment he went to see one of his closest friends, Abusha, to get some advice since his friend served in that region under the previous administration.

Abusha was happy to learn that his friend was appointed as the Governor in the province he served previously. He advised Shumiye that there are certain local norms and traditions which he must conform to, until he was accepted by the local people. The province of Gayint, especially, has a different way of life and the expectations of local people are considerably different from that of the rest of the country.

The Governor Goes Crazy

Shumiye responded "Oh! you! You are trying to reflect your sentiments of the past. For me there is nothing to be learnt from the past. I will go as a simple man, dress simply, I will take nobody with me when I make field visits, I shall stay for some time in a hotel and then move to the villa meant for Governor's residence. I will cook my own food." Abusha could not believe the attitude of his friend. He tried to explain to Shumiye the dangers of ignoring the local cultural values and expectations, especially during the period of adjustment to the new place.

Without heeding the advice of his friend, Shumiye left for his new job with a great determination to radically change the place and people. However, he ignored the fact that people in the Gayint province belonged to the Amhora tribe, who consider themselves the original and prominent Ethiopians. They have their own pride in maintaining their traditions and customs.

Traditionally, when the new Governor reports to a province, people will be informed of his visit and get ready to greet him since a certain amount of dignity goes with the office of the Governor. Nobody was informed of Shumiye's coming. He went to Gayint by public transportation. Local people were rather shocked and surprised to see him in his office. They had a difficult time figuring out whether he was a Governor or a strange imposter since this had happened before. People thought that he should have sent a message prior to his arrival, informing them of his expected time of arrival and the things which he needed done.

After staying in a hotel for a few days, Shumiye moved to a villa meant for Governor's residence. Once settled, he contemplated moving to a small and ordinary house in order to identify with the local people. He made some enquiries on renting such a place. But the word already got around that the "new man", the so-called Governor, planned to live in a hut.

Since the food stocks he had brought along with him were exhausted, he planned to shop for groceries. As there was no one available to buy things for him and to cook his food, he himself went to the market with his bamboo bag to buy chicken and eggs. People could not believe their eyes when they saw their Governor with a bamboo bag, chickens and eggs. A series of such things were happening, exhibiting the simple behavior of the Governor. On seeing these, people doubted the sanity — let alone capability — of the new government in appointing

Culture and Management: A Casebook

people for such high offices. They started to cast their doubts on the so-called "People's Revolution".

After a while, Shumiye felt the need for personal transportation and went to the market to buy a mule. Putting a considerable effort in bargaining, he bought a mule and pulled it himself to his home. Before this, he never had riding lessons. He had to spend some time daily, collecting grass in order to feed his mule. About three months after buying the mule and learning a few riding lessons, Shumiye rode to Tach Gayint, one of the districts in his province for a field visit. Upon reaching the place, he tied his mule to a tree closer to the marketplace as he felt that it was the best opportunity to get the attention of people without bothering them to come for a meeting on working days to his office. Then he climbed on a huge rock and clapped his hands to draw the attention of people. But nobody paid any attention to him since the local people could not recognize him as their Provincial Governor. Even those who recognized him did not bother to listen to him. They only took pity on him for his abnormal behavior. They whispered to each other, saying, "Look at this insane person who is unfit to be our Governor, "*Aifo ayawouk deha*".

The news spread around and people started to blame the government for sending such a sick person to be their Governor. They considered this as an insult to the entire population of the province. A few representatives were sent to the headquarters in Adis Abada to convey the feelings of people in the province and their reaction to the newly appointed Governor. They wanted their messengers to inform the government authorities and the Revolutionary Council that if the Governor was not removed immediately, there will be a revolt.

The members of the Revolutionary Council were jolted by this incident. They were worried that this incident might be the first of many problems from other provinces. If so, their socialist plans and programs would be in jeopardy. On one hand, they did not want to give in to the demands of people and transfer Shumiye to some other province. On the other hand, they did not want to see a mini-revolution against the state and its socialistic ideology. They had to react without much delay.